WILLOW

Reaktion's Botanical series is the first of its kind, integrating horticultural and botanical writing with a broader account of the cultural and social impact of trees, plants and flowers.

WILLOW

Alison Syme

REAKTION BOOKS

To the willowy Miranda

Published by
REAKTION BOOKS LTD
33 Great Sutton Street
London EC1V 0DX, UK

www.reaktionbooks.co.uk

First published 2014

Copyright © Alison Syme 2014

Printed and bound in China by Toppan Printing Co., Ltd

A catalogue record for this book is available from the British Library

ISBN 978 1 78023 292 8

Contents

꩜

Salix fragilis (crack willow) pollard, Thame, Oxfordshire.

Introduction: Natural History

H aunters of waterways and hedgerow guardians, jewels of the garden and common sallies of the fields, willows are at once the most poetic and practical of plants. Different species exhibit seemingly every possible physical characteristic – from towering to tiny, bright to pale, languid to erect – and the uses to which they have been put are as wide-ranging as their forms. For millennia humans have woven willow baskets, furniture, fences and walls. We have treated illnesses with willow and incorporated it into myths and rituals, from celebrations of fertility to funerary rites. And of course willows have been valued for their beauty and poetic resonance: from the Far East to the Far West, they have adorned gardens and featured as a recurring motif in art and literature. Monet painted them again and again, and willow was one of Shakespeare's favourite tropes of tragic love. Perhaps it is the very variety of willow's forms and functions that has led to its assuming such a key, and yet contra-dictory, place in our imagination. Linked, as we shall see, with life and death, grief and joy, toil and play, necessity and ornament, willow has, in different times and places, functioned as a mirror of and partici-pant in almost every aspect of human existence. It is our intimate familiar, and this book will unfold the ways in which the fate of this tree of tears, of dreams, of love and of death has always been bound up with our own.

Pussy willow.

Willows belong to the *Salicaceae* family of flowering plants. Their genus, *Salix*, contains between 350 and 500 astonishingly diverse species, from the loftiest weeping varieties with their graceful pendant tresses to cropped willows sprouting shocks of brightly coloured branches to ground-hugging arctic dwarfs. These may produce long and thin or short and round leaves, and stems that are straight or spiralling in a rainbow of colours. But whether tree, shrub or creeper, most of these plants produce distinctive catkins: emerging from grey, downy buds (pussy willows) – one of the first signs of spring – catkins are thin, cylindrical, soft, hairy clusters of flowers. They bloom in a wide spectrum of colours and sizes, from the bright red of some *Salix purpurea* to the rich black of *S. melanostachys* to yellows, purples, pinks and greens. Willows are almost all dioecious (producing only male or female flowers on one plant), and the range of catkin colours

Salix purpurea male catkin.

is further nuanced when the anthers on the male flowers open in stages to reveal their yellow pollen.

The word *Salix* derives from the Celtic *sallis*, *sal* (near) + *lis* (water), and if many willows like to live near water, they have also, historically, travelled along it. Angiosperms, or flowering plants, first appeared during the relatively warm period of the Cretaceous, 65 to 145 million years ago. Fossilized *Salix* pollen and leaf fragments from this era indicate that dwarf willows, pollinated by honeybees and other insects, made up a significant portion of Cretaceous flora. Originating in the mountains of East Asia, *Salix* species appear to have spread across the northern hemisphere when the glaciers of the most recent glacial period melted and formed rivers carrying sediment. While willows largely grow in temperate and arctic regions, species thrive in an array of habitats: lush river valleys, deserts, tropics, tundra and mountains,

Salix melanostachys catkins.

some growing at elevations of over 4,000 m in the Himalayas. Most are distributed above the equator, with the greatest numbers in Asia, Europe and North America, and smaller populations in North Africa and India. There are a few indigenous species in South America, primarily *S. humboldtiana*; *S. mucronata* (silver willow) is native to southern Africa.[1]

These world travellers are so numerous and varied in form that *Salix* species are often grouped into subgenuses: 'true willows' (large trees and tall shrubs, subgenus *Salix*), osiers and sallows (small trees and shrubs, subgenus *Caprisalix*), and dwarfs (subgenus *Chamaetia*). The 'true willows' include *S. alba* (white willow), *S. babylonica* (weeping willow), *S. fragilis* (crack willow) and other trees and large shrubs whose branches may be pendulous or upright. Preferring to grow in river valleys, these trees can reach heights of 25 m and attain impressive girths; an 80-year-old willow can rival a 300-year-old oak in proportions.[2] If pollarded – their tops removed to promote a regular, harvestable

Salix alba 'Vitelina-Tristis' (golden weeping willow), Toronto, Canada.

Weeping willow in Dazhai, Shanxi Province, China.

growth of pliable branches called withies – they live longer than they would otherwise (willows' quick growth results in top-heavy trees liable to split) and provide food and shade for livestock, firewood and materials for agricultural implements. Rows of pollards with their thick, gnarled trunks may be seen skirting fields, drainage ditches and canals all over Europe, where in the past willows were, as one nineteenth-century writer lamented, 'so universally subject to . . . pollarding, for the purpose of providing stakes and hurdles for the farm, that probably few persons [had] ever seen a willow tree.'[3] Pollarded willows form richer habitats for other wildlife than any other tree: birds nest in their open crowns or are drawn to the hundreds of species of insects that live in the detritus-catching tops.[4]

Osiers and sallows (or sallies) include *S. viminalis* (common osier) and *S. caprea* (goat willow), and are smaller than true willows, rarely taller than 6 m. These species are wasteland colonizers; most thrive in damp soils, but some will grow in dry and sandy soils and can be used to fix sand dunes. Osiers tend to have long, narrow leaves and sallows broader, rounded ones, but such distinctions are loose. Species within this group of willows provide the pussy willow branches so common in

Pollards near Haastrecht, South Holland, the Netherlands.

Salix fragilis (crack willow) pollards, Britwell Salome, Oxfordshire.

Salix caprea (goat willow), Dancersend Nature Reserve, Buckinghamshire.

Easter festivities and the sometimes brightly coloured withies used for basket-making and other essential rustic crafts — 'for all *Wicker* and *Twiggie* works', as one seventeenth-century gardener put it.[5] The swarming root networks of osiers help fortify banks and prevent erosion, for which reason they are frequently planted along watercourses.

Dwarf willows are hardy creeping or trailing shrubs not more than a metre in height and frequently just a few centimetres tall; they have small, often rounded leaves and spread horizontally. A number of species grow far above the treeline, making them the northernmost woody plants. They are adapted to conditions of severe exposure on mountains and in the Arctic, where they are an essential part of the diet of arctic hare, caribou, muskox and other animals. Botanists have disagreed over whether *Salix* contains a third subgenus, *Chosenia*, and indeed the history of *Salix* is inseparable from the difficulties inherent in its classification.

In combination with the vast geographical area across which the genus has spread and the diversity of species within it, the natural hybridization that frequently occurs makes classification a challenge. Linnaeus considered willows 'extremely difficult to classify',[6] and William Hooker agreed that they were exceedingly slippery:

Salix alba var. *vitellina*, Grobelno, Slovenia.

Arctic willow in Alaska.

there is not in the whole range of the vegetable creation, a genus, liable to more variation at different periods of growth, in different soils and situations, and under different circumstances; so that the accurate determination of its species has baffled the searches of the ablest botanists.[7]

Contemporary biologists agree that identification of this polymorphous plant can be tricky; even genetic analysis is not fully reliable, as members of the same species may exhibit chromosomal variations.[8] The word willow comes from Anglo-Saxon *welig*, meaning pliancy, and it is indeed a supple, not to say shifty, class of plant.

Early accounts of *Salix* stressed willow's applications rather than its botanical features. Roman writers including Pliny, Cato and Varro enumerated its agricultural uses, from tying up grapevines to basketry. Cato ranked the osier field (*salictum*) one of the most valuable parts of a farm, following only the vineyard and the garden and preceding even the olive grove.[9] Pliny considered willow 'the most useful of the water-plants',[10] and provided instructions on its planting, raising and pollarding. In his fourteenth-century *Liber ruralium commodorum* (Book of Rural Benefits), Pietro de' Crescenzi added some personal observations to those of the ancients but did not offer detailed descriptions of the plants; a woodcut illustration from a fifteenth-century edition shows a pollarded osier at the edge of a stream, its springy, leafy rods suggesting both strength and suppleness but not offering enough visual information to identify a particular species.

In the sixteenth and seventeenth centuries, authors of herbals and agricultural treatises provided more botanically precise appreciations of willows without neglecting their practical virtues. John Gerard's *Herbal* of 1597 lists 'divers sorts' under 'sundry titles' including 'the Oziar, the Sallow, the Rose Willow, the common Withie, and the Dwarffe Willow' and discusses the bark, roots, leaves and basic shapes of each. The common willow, for example, has leaves that are 'long, lesser, and narrower than those of the Peach tree, somewhat greene on the upper side and slipperie, and on the nether side softer and whiter',

'*Salix*', in Pietro de' Crescenzi, *Ruralia Commoda* (Speier, 1490); and '*Salix*', in John
Gerard, *The Herbal* (London, 1597).

and its boughs are 'covered with either a purple or else a white barke'.
Gerard and other contemporary writers noted the differences between
willow catkins – some 'long and mossie', others 'round' – and the 'white
and soft down' attached to the willow seeds, which 'bears them away
with the wind'.[11] (Pliny had observed that 'the fruit of the willow
before maturity develops a kind of cobweb'.[12])

In *Sylva; or, A Discourse of Forest-Trees*, first published in 1664, John
Evelyn offered a longer list of willow types and varieties within them;
he broke down sallies, for example, into the 'vulgar', the 'hopping' and
the kind having 'twigs *reddish*', though he was stymied by the 'innumer-
able' sorts of osiers. He discussed the soil each type prefers (common
willows 'delight in *Meads* and *Ditch-sides*' not over-wet) and provided
an extensive list of applications: the third year's growth of a pollarded
sallow is 'strong enough to make *Rakes*, and *Pike-staves*', the fourth year's
a plough; osier wands may be used for cradles and chairs in addition
to beehives, lattices, hurdles and hoops. Evelyn even suggested an

application for the downy fluff attached to wind-born willow seeds: when the seeds are released in great clouds by sallows, a 'poor Body might in an hours space gather a pound or two of [the fluff], which resembling the finest silk, might doubtless be put to some profitable use by an ingenious house-wife',[13] as it is by some birds, who line their nests with the soft stuff.

In the nineteenth century willow still ranked, according to William Hooker, 'among the first in our list of œconomical plants',[14] and it was studied by a number of prominent botanists. James Russell, Duke of Bedford, planted a *salictum*, a collection of different varieties of *Salix*, at his estate of Woburn Abbey. His gardener, James Forbes, compiled a catalogue and suggested some of the difficulties involved in identifying willows, which need to be studied at different times of the spring and summer, when the leaves (which change shape and size) are young and when they are mature, and when the catkins have emerged. Forbes's catalogue attests to the range of willow species and their varied colouring; he describes 'violet-coloured willow' as a 'small *tree*, with dark violet-covered *branches*, slender, drooping, covered all over with a violet powder like a plum' and unfolds for the reader a willow spectrum: bitter purple, blue, brown-branched, white, dark green, golden, grey, pale, rose, violet-coloured, white.[15]

Although willows were more precisely classified and described in the nineteenth century, often at great length by botanists like J. C. Loudon, they were still frequently mystifying. William Scaling, Queen Victoria's basket-maker, was perplexed by particular species names. *S. viminalis*, derived from *vimen*, Latin for twig, irked him, for 'it is about the least twiggy of any kind, and as a rule, it grows perfectly smooth, straight, and clear of twigs, or side branches'. And *S. purpurea*, which is not always purple, represents 'only one of the apparently inextricable muddles in which the whole genus Salix is involved'.[16] Willow's various names, though, are the least of its mysteries; as we will see, it is associ-ated with the underworld, magic and the moon. In his *Complete Herbal* of 1653, the English botanist and physician Nicholas Culpeper declared with certainty, 'The moon owns it.'[17] And despite his agronomical

Sorted withies. Lakeshore Willows, Ontario.

and botanical empiricism, John Evelyn advised planting and cutting willows at the new moon.[18]

The willow's perceived connection with the underworld and the supernatural are in part due to one of its modes of reproduction, for willows reproduce both sexually and vegetatively. After the buds have lengthened and become flowery catkins, they lure a variety of insects, though willows are primarily pollinated by honeybees. Later the female catkins launch hosts of minuscule seeds, 'the most buoyant of the seeds of any of our trees' according to Thoreau, which float 'the most like gossamer of any, in a meandering manner' on the wind. Their

Willow catkins,
in *Les Grandes Heures
d'Anne de Bretagne,*
c. 1500, manuscript
illumination.

imminent transformation is astonishing to think of: 'some of these
downy atoms, which strike your cheek without your being conscious
of it, may come to be pollards five feet in diameter'.[19] It is willows'
vegetative reproduction, however, that is, to some, uncanny. Apparently dead fallen twigs, encountering soil and water, will put down
roots, their vital force seemingly insuperable. Some willows reproduce
exclusively vegetatively, such as the aptly named crack willow which splits
down the middle if its upper boughs become too heavy and whose
branches are fragile enough to break in the wind; if the fallen twigs
land in a watercourse they can travel far before they land and root.[20]
Such flexible parts are characteristic of the whole genus; as Loudon
put it, the willow's 'roots are more readily changed into branches,
and the branches into roots, than in any other species of a tree'.[21] This
mutability translates into longevity. Most willow trees have relatively
short lifespans – 50–70 or maybe 100 years – although there is a
nearly 300-year-old white willow in Aptekarsky Ogorod in Moscow (a
garden for medicinal plants founded in 1706 by Peter the Great), and
some sexually reproducing willow species, like *S. caprea* (goat willow),
can live up to 500 years. Vegetatively reproducing trees, however, are
potentially immortal.[22]

Popular etymologies of the various names of willows emphasize their vivacity. The medieval etymologist Isidore of Seville incorrectly derived *Salix* from the Latin *salire*, to jump, explaining that it 'is so called because it swiftly "springs up" (*salire*), that is, quickly grows'. He also thought the term *vimen* (osier) was due to the plant's 'great intensity (*vis*, accusative *vim*) of greenness'.[23] Thoreau captured something of the speed of osiers' growth in his description of it:

> How impatient, how rampant, how precocious these osiers.
> . . . They have hardly made two shoots from the sand in as many
> springs, when silvery catkins burst out along them, and anon
> golden blossoms and downy seeds, spreading their race with
> an incredible rapidity.[24]

This life force was thought to be transmittable to humans. According to European folklore, a newborn injured during delivery should be passed through the freshly cleft trunk or branch of a willow, which would then be tied shut; when the tree grew together again, the child would be healed.[25] Similarly, a child suffering from rickets could be 'passed through a cleft in a willow tree' to cure it. A rather sneaky Flemish 'cure' for ague was 'to go early in the morning to an old willow, tie three knots in one of its branches, say "Good-morrow, Old One, I give thee the cold; good-morrow, Old One," then turn and run away without looking round'.[26] Such magical remedies aside, virtually every culture in the northern hemisphere has included willow in its repertoire of medicinal plants.

In 1763 the Reverend Edward Stone presented a paper on the medicinal application of the bark of the common white willow (*S. alba*) to the Royal Society of London. Having chewed some on a walk one day, he was inspired to investigate the accounts in old herbals of willow bark's virtue. He collected a pound of bark by stripping the shoots of pollarded white willows, then slowly dried and powdered it. Mixed with 'water, tea, small beer and such like', he served it, over the next five years, to 50 people suffering from agues, concluding that

Salix fragilis (crack willow) pollard, Nether Winchendon, Buckinghamshire.

it was a safe and effective medicine.[27] Sixty-five years later, in 1828, the German chemist Johann Andreas Buchner managed to extract from willow bark a yellow substance which he named salicin, after *Salix*. Over the next two decades chemists analysed salicin from willow and other plants, which oxidizes in the body to become salicylic acid. In

Salix alba (white willow) leaves and bark.

1897 Felix Hoffmann, a chemist at Bayer, synthesized acetylsalicylic acid and, in 1899, it was registered as Aspirin.[28]

Physicians of the Greco-Roman world prescribed *Salix* for a variety of ailments. In the fifth century BCE Hippocrates recommended that pregnant women chew willow leaves during childbirth to relieve pain and to treat post-partum fever. The first-century Greek physician Dioscorides suggested a decoction of its leaves and bark to treat ear-aches, gout and dandruff in his *De Materia Medica*, also noting that the leaves, beaten and mixed with pepper and wine, cure gas.[29] According to Pliny, the 'juice' of the willow is useful for 'clearing away humours that obstruct the eye' and 'for promoting urine and for draining outwards all gatherings'; 'ash from the burnt bark of the tips of the branches' mixed with water removes 'corns and callosities'.[30]

Willow became a standard entry in Western herbals in the Middle Ages and Renaissance. These texts are often recyclings of Dioscorides,

Illustration from Jiang Tingxi, ed., *Gu jin tu shu ji cheng mu lu* (Shanghai, 1934).

though sometimes they augment the minimal instructions and recipes of the ancients; the second part of William Turner's *New Herball* of 1561, for example, advises that the burnt willow bark used to treat corns and other 'hard lumps and little swellings' should be soaked with vinegar and laid on as a plaster.[31] Culpeper recommends the 'water that is gathered from the willow' by slitting the bark 'when it flowereth' for 'redness and dimness of sight', and prescribes willow leaves, bark and seeds to staunch bleeding and stop vomiting.[32]

The tannins and salicin in willow account for its efficacy in treating diarrhoea, bleeding, pain, fever and fluid retention.[33] One of the most enduring beliefs about willow's medicinal properties – that it is a contraceptive – has not been scientifically demonstrated and is curious given willow's vitality. Dioscorides wrote that willow leaves, mixed with water, 'cause inconception', and Pliny warned that too many doses of the pounded leaves in drink would cause 'absolute impotence'.[34] Scholars have argued that these ideas are traceable to Homer's description of willows as 'fruit-losing' or 'fruit-destroying' in book ten of *The Odyssey*.[35] The epithet stuck, and writers all over Europe and the Middle East offered recipes for contraceptives and abortifacients that included willow. Willow seed, according to Pliny, 'produces barrenness in a woman',[36] and Galen's prescriptions for emmenagogues (menstruation-stimulating drugs) include willow. The fourth-century Greek physician Oribasius recommended a post-coital drink of willow leaves and fern root for women to prevent conception, while the sixth-century Byzantine doctor Aëtius of Amida advised men to drink a mixture of 'the burned testicles of castrated mules' and willow. A number of ninth- to eleventh-century Arabic works by Rhazes (Muhammed ibn Zakariya al-Razi), Abu al-Hasan al-Tabib and Avicenna (ibn Sina) likewise list willow contraceptives and abortifacients.[37]

In China the white willow (*S. alba*) has been used since at least 500 BCE to treat pain and fever.[38] A second-century pharmacopoeia, *Shen Nong Ben Cao Jing*, describes willow as a bitter and cold plant suitable for reducing inflammation and recommends a preparation of willow bark for arthritis, perhaps because its gnarled trunks evoked the tortured joints of sufferers. It also prescribes willow seeds ground into a powder for jaundice or to stop bleeding; willow root for unwonted vaginal discharges; willow branch as an analgesic; and willow leaves for mastitis, goitre, swelling and skin diseases.[39] Li Shizhen's *Ben Cao Gang Mu* of 1578, a Ming text considered the definitive compendium of materia medica, lists stewed *S. babylonica* leaves as good for scabies and malignant sores, and stewed root bark for jaundice and 'whitish and turbid urine' as well as swelling and flatulence. Stewed *S. purpurea* twigs, furthermore, are recommended for carbuncles and smallpox. In a rare piece of dental advice, willow twigs are suggested as toothbrushes.[40]

In addition to treating aches and pains, willow has also, for thousands of years, been used in trauma medicine. One of the case studies in the Edwin Smith Papyrus, an ancient Egyptian surgical treatise dated to *c.* 1500 BCE, describes an infected chest wound to which willow leaves are first applied to reduce the inflammation before any other treatment is undertaken.[41] Medieval Japanese medical treatises similarly advised the use of willow in combination with other plant substances to treat battle injuries: the *Kíhō* of 1391 (Demon Formulas) suggests treating deep cuts to the hands or feet by applying red bean powder to the wound and then wrapping it in 'a weave of willow', while *Kínsō ryōjíshō* (On Healing Incised Wounds) of 1357 directs the medic to place willow wood that has been wrapped in cloth and steamed below cuts to the bone while shaving rattan palm resin into the wounds.[42] And in the nineteenth and early twentieth centuries, when mechanized warfare and modern medicine meant an increase in the number of veterans with lost limbs, willow became the wood of choice for prostheses.

Two unusual willow remedies are worth citing for curiosity's sake. The Roman medical encyclopaedist Aulus Cornelius Celsus, writing around 30 CE, advised the use of willow leaves in the case of anal or vaginal prolapse: after bathing the protruding tissue in salt water or dry wine, he advised, it should be reinserted into the orifice, then 'willow leaves boiled in vinegar applied, next lint, and wool over it: and these must be bandaged on, whilst the legs are kept tied together'.[43] And the Mawangdui medical manuscripts – seven third- and early second-century BCE texts found in a Chinese tomb – prescribe an ointment of beaten willow catkins and rancid lard to reduce swollen genitals.[44]

These medical examples suggest how intimately willow was part of our lives in previous centuries. And although we may not be aware

Artificial leg, 1901–40, willow and leather.

Salix psammophila (sand willow) in Ordos, Inner Mongolia, China.

of it, willow plays an increasingly important role today. *Salix* species are being used across the northern hemisphere to rehabilitate soils and mediate some of the destruction humans continue to wreak on the planet. *S. psammophila* (sand willow) and other species work, in Inner Mongolia and elsewhere, to combat desertification, while willow plantations in Europe treat sewage, landfill and other wastewater, their roots absorbing nitrogen and other undesirable substances.[45] In addition to biofiltration, willow is used in bioengineering: soil, slope and bank stabilization as well as constructed wetlands. Coppiced willow is an increasingly common fast-growing, high-yield biofuel which needs little fertilizer, burns cleanly and, compared to other arable crops, harbours a wide variety of different plant species as well as birds, butter -flies, bees and other insects.[46] Our sustained relationship with willow may teach us to forge a sustainable relationship with the environment in general.

We have largely lost touch, though, with willow and its meanings. This book aims to reacquaint us. If willow is geographically widespread and hugely variable in form, its cultural history is equally rich, complex and global. As we will see, its names in other languages link it to earth as well as water, to poetry, sorrow, madness and even war. It is a figure of journeys, bridging East and West, life and death, joy and grief. We will trace its roots in myth, magic, ritual and religion across the northern hemisphere, from ancient Egypt to the present day, and examine the functional and beautiful objects and architectures it has inspired. The curious and convoluted history of the willow pattern plate, the world's most popular china pattern, will open up new perspectives on an under-appreciated mass medium and our most intimate domestic scenes. Reading into willow's place in literature will shed new light on the way we commemorate loss and love, and work through trauma; and discovering the willow's essential place in art will open new sightlines into old pictures. Finally, we will explore what may have seemed the most obvious place to begin: the willow in the garden, where it serves, in addition to aesthetic and practical ends, as an imaginary bridge between times and places.

one

Rites of Spring and Mourning

૱

Willow has been thought of as emblematic of life force, and even of immortality, but it has also long been linked with death, the underworld and witches. Its symbolic ambiguity is in part due to its remarkable resilience: what appear to be dead, fallen branches take root easily and produce new growths, offering a seemingly magical vision of the renewal of life in death. When the velvety, pale grey buds of the goat willow burst into yellow pollen, changing silver into gold, a similarly dramatic transmutation occurs. The genus *Salix* has fulfilled a remarkable range of symbolic functions, and this chapter will explore willow's place in the mythic, magical, religious and even political beliefs and practices of diverse cultures.

In the ancient world, willow was associated with both life and death. In Egypt, the willow or *tcheret* (*Salix safsaf*) was sacred to Osiris, god of the dead. Osiris was murdered by his brother Set, tricked into entering a chest which was then sealed and set adrift on the Nile. It came to rest under a willow tree, in the boughs of which the soul of the drowned god perched and sang in the form of a bird. When Set subsequently dismembered Osiris and spread his body parts around Egypt, the places where the pieces were buried (before Isis gathered them together and resurrected her brother) became associated with willow groves. As a symbol of both death and rebirth, Osiris and willow were identified with the moon and the harvest, with their cyclical disappearances and returns. To ensure the fertility of the land each year, the Egyptians celebrated a festival called 'raising the willow'.[1]

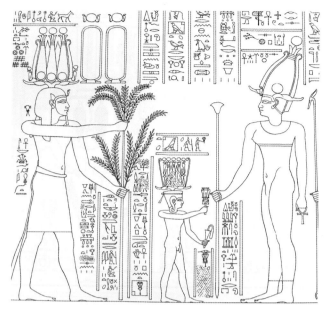

Pharaoh offering willow branches in the temple of Hathor at Dendera, in Auguste Mariette-Bey, *Dendérah: description générale du grand temple de cette ville* (Paris, 1870).

A ritual formula inscribed in the temple of the goddess Hathor at Dendera (which was also called Nikentori or Nitentori, meaning willow wood or willow earth) was spoken when the offering was made 'at the beginning of the first month of the season of summer': 'I offer you the willow. I raise before you this branch in the temple of the sistrum. We make the feast of drunkenness in the place you love.' A relief from a column in the inner hypostyle hall shows a pharaoh raising a slim, leafy willow in offering to the goddess whose devotees, during the festival, wore willow crowns and garlands.[2]

In ancient Greece, the willow was also identified with the dead and deities. Homer's 'fruit-destroying willows' grew in the groves of Persephone in Hades, and when Orpheus descended into the underworld to find Eurydice, his dead wife, he carried willow wands. Some have suggested that these preserved him 'from the fiends',[3] others that the branches of the chthonic tree served as a guide to the mysterious realms beneath the earth. Deadly women were linked with willows;

the trees were sacred to the goddess/witch Hecate, and the beautiful enchantress Circe, who transformed Odysseus' crew into animals, lived amidst 'a thick weird grove of funereal Willows in the island of Æææa',[4] where she sometimes hung the corpses of men in their upper boughs.[5]

Willow was also linked with Demeter, the goddess of agriculture, and Dionysus, the god of wine. Dionysus carried a thyrsus or wand, the base of which was sometimes said to be made of willow. And in a frieze in the Villa of the Mysteries in Pompeii, dedicated to the cult of Dionysus, a fertility symbol in the form of a giant phallus whose shape is faintly visible beneath a veil is set in a willow *liknon*,

Bacchante lifting the veil covering a fertility symbol in a willow *liknon*, 1st century CE, fresco. Villa of the Mysteries, Pompeii.

or harvest basket. During the festivals of Demeter, the *Vitex agnus-castus*, which was believed to be a variety of willow, was strewn on the ground to make beds for women. This custom was originally practised to promote fertility but later changed significance and became a 'dedication to chastity', a paradox sustainable by the willow's dual signification, in the Greek world, as 'mother and virgin, fruitful and chaste, living and dead'.[6]

In the Judaeo-Christian tradition, the account in Psalm 137 of the exiled Israelites hanging their harps on willows and weeping has long linked the tree with grief: 'By the rivers of Babylon – there we sat down and there we wept when we remembered Zion. On the willows there we hung up our harps.'[7] Although some modern editions correct 'willows' to 'poplars' (the trees growing by the rivers of Babylon were, apparently, *Populus euphratica*),[8] the willow's mournful signification has endured: nineteenth-century dictionaries of the language of flowers give its meaning as 'forsaken'.[9] In the Jewish tradition, however, the willow is not only a symbol of loss and exile; it also signifies joy, prosperity and blessing in the Feast of Tabernacles (*Sukkot*), described in Leviticus 23. This celebration, one day of which is called the Day of the Willows, begins on the fifteenth day of the seventh month in the Jewish calendar – in September or October – and is a curious splicing together of an autumn harvest festival (Dionysus, whose mystery cult was linked in various ways with willow, was worshipped in Jerusalem in the first century BCE) and a commemoration of the Jews' forty years of wandering in the desert. For the week of the feast's duration, celebrants construct tabernacles or *sukkah*, little huts roofed with palm and 'willows of the brook' in remembrance of the tents or other shelters in which the exiled Jews dwelt; in these temporary structures they take their meals and, in some cases, sleep. Willow branches are used to bless the earth and, on the seventh day, the ground is beaten with willows during the great Hosanna (a full prayer cycle) until their leaves fall off.

Willow was one of several plants whose symbolic qualities served as a bridge between Greco-Roman myth and Christianity. For early Christians and those of the Middle Ages, it became a symbol of the

Blessing of the pussy willows on Palm Sunday in Blaichach, Germany, 2012.

'chastity that dies unto itself and thus becomes eternally fruitful', of a life of purity and its heavenly reward.[10] *Vitex agnus-castus*, which was still believed to be a willow in the Middle Ages, was used to make protective girdles by monks who supposed its withies could repel all unclean thoughts. According to some sources, this practice endured until the eighteenth century.[11] *Salix*, however, also had (and still has) a much more visible place in Christian ritual.

Palm Sunday, the Sunday before Easter, celebrates Christ's entry into Jerusalem and is named after the palm fronds thrown down before him by the people, according to the Gospel of John. In various Central and Eastern European Catholic and Orthodox churches Palm Sunday is known as Willow or Pussy Willow Sunday, and pussy willows are substituted for palm fronds in church and local rituals. Because willow catkins are one of the first signs of spring – and willow, as we have seen, may appear dead and then spring to life – budding branches are a suitable figure for the Resurrection. On Willow Sunday, then, from Bavaria to Russia, congregants bring willow branches to church to be blessed, and sometimes then process through the village or town, after which they may be placed in houses, cowsheds and fields to ward off sickness, death and evil. The 'common people of Europe', the German folklorist Wilhelm Mannhardt tells us, thought of willows as 'demon destroyers' because they emblematized life force and, once blessed, the power of the Christian deity.[12]

Pussy willows were placed behind icons and in the corners of stables to function apotropaically. They were also used more actively in the expulsion of evil: all over Central and Eastern Europe switches or whips woven out of budded willow wands were used to beat both people and animals. To be fully effective the wands needed to be covered with young catkins (in Germany, if the willows had not budded before Willow Sunday they were placed in warm water or even in the oven to force the process). After the blessing of the branches young men thrashed people while shouting, 'The willow is beating you, not me!' Such whippings took place throughout the week leading up to Easter Sunday, sometimes targeting those who had missed church, but more generally women, children and cows. As epilepsy was believed by some to be the result of demonic possession, in some parts of Europe epileptics were beaten with freshly cut willow branches at Easter to drive out evil spirits. In the south of Germany a superstition, still alive in the nineteenth century, held that three catkins of blessed willows thrown into the fire or swallowed staved off lightning strikes, while in Russia the poor ate a porridge made from catkins to internalize the blessing.[13]

On Easter Monday or St George's day (23 April), Roma in Transylvania and Romania celebrated the coming of spring with the festival of 'Green George'. The evening before, a young willow would be cut down, decorated with garlands and erected somewhere in the encampment. Pregnant women would place an article of clothing beneath it and if by the next morning a willow leaf had fallen anywhere on the garment they could look forward to an easy delivery. The elderly and infirm also visited the willow on the eve of the festival to spit on it and beg 'you will soon die, but let us live', for the willow was believed able to impart something of its 'vital energy' to supplicants. On St George's day itself, a boy completely covered in foliage and flowers became 'Green

George', the 'human double of the tree' who distributed the blessings of earth and water. He fed the animals to ensure they would be nourished throughout the year, then took three iron nails which had 'lain for three days and nights in water', hammered them into the willow, removed them and threw them into a stream 'to propitiate the water-spirits'. Finally, a further double of Green George himself – a puppet – was thrown into the water.[14] In this Christianized fertility rite, the nailed and suffering, Christ-like willow offered extended, if not eternal, life to its worshippers.

May Day celebrations throughout Europe also involved willow structures and implements. In various parts of Germany and France, people planted leafy willow poles decorated with flowers and danced around them.[15] In England, a figure similar to Green George called 'Jack-in-the-Green' donned a pyramidal wicker framework covered with holly, ivy, flowers and ribbons, and danced through the village or town at the head of a line.[16] A mid-nineteenth-century watercolour (see overleaf) shows a procession of dancers including a Lord of May and the tilting figure of Jack-in-the-Green. A view hole allows him to see out, though some contemporary accounts describe the willow framework as so 'covered with green leaves and bunches of flowers interwoven with each other . . . that the man within may be completely concealed'.[17]

During the month of May, willow symbolized the growth of friendship and love. In Romania, friends cut a silver coin in half so each could keep a part, ate and drank together, took an oath, and then went into the fields with 'two circlets of plaited willow'. Holding these before their faces, they exchanged 'a kiss of communion' through them and then crowned each other below the oldest local tree in flower. Men cut down leafy branches of willow and planted these 'love Mays' in front of their houses.[18] In Bohemia, more active expressions of affection were preferred. Girls made 'summers' – willow wands woven together with ribbons – with which they beat unsuspecting young men. Wives also beat their husbands with summers, crying 'Give me Give me Give me!', and young boys carried catkin-loaded willow branches to use as whips.[19]

Jack-in-the-Green
procession, c. 1840,
watercolour.

Willow's manifold ritual functions are not only a Western phenomenon. In the East, it plays an important role in Buddhism and
is associated with water, tears and mercy. Avalokitesvara, the bodhisattva of compassion, is frequently depicted holding a willow branch
with which he may sprinkle 'sweet dew' upon sufferers. In China,
the bodhisattva, called Guanyin, can be depicted as male or female
and is particularly associated with healing, sprinkling the 'nectar of
life on the sick and dying' with willow branches.[20] A tenth-century
painting shows a male Guanyin seated beneath a stand of bamboo, foot
resting on a lotus, and holding a willow branch with which he may
rain down mercy on a supplicant below. Guanyin is also frequently
shown holding a *kundika*, a type of water sprinkler used in Buddhist
ceremonies to define or consecrate sacred space and for other purification rites.[21] These vessels, which are filled with water through a
spout in the side and sprinkle it out through a long neck, are often
decorated with willows. A twelfth-century Korean celadon example

Detail of
Avalokitesvara/Guanyin,
c. 926–75.

(see overleaf) has a beautiful pale green, translucent, crackled glaze which reads as a rippled watery surface; on one side swimming ducks are inlaid, on the other, a willow.

A similar form of healing willow sprinkling was practised by the Ainu, an indigenous people of Japan: during solar eclipses they dipped willow branches in water and made to sprinkle the vanished sun in a gesture of healing.[22] The Ainu also offered whittled willow sticks to their gods,[23] and many Shinto ceremonies use implements made from willow. Historically, ceremonial hats were decorated with willow branches to pray for happiness. An eleventh-century Japanese treatise on gardening recommends planting willows in all gardens, but especially those with ponds, as willows were often believed to be transformed water spirits. By the same logic, willows were planted near wells where they reputedly helped people get water. Willows played a less merciful role on New Year's Day in the Heian period (794–1185), when married but childless women were beaten with willow sticks to make them conceive male children. There are records of women dying from severe willow beatings, but over time the custom became more moderate, apparently, more like a 'pat'.[24]

In both East and West, willow has been used in practices of divination ranging from prophecy to dream interpretation. According to Herodotus, Scythian soothsayers foretold the future with willow sticks: they laid out willow rods from a bundle on the ground one by one and then gathered them into the bundle again, all the while speaking a prophesy.[25] The Mongols and their predecessors also practised willow divination,[26] and it has been suggested that the first sticks for the *Yi Jing* were willow twigs rather than yarrow stalks. Chen Shiyuan, the author of a sixteenth-century encyclopaedia of dream interpretation, refers to an ancient technique called the 'long-willow method', the details of which are no longer known.[27] Willow seems to have been widely linked with the ability to sort out dreams: Native American dreamcatchers were traditionally made of a willow hoop across which a web of sinew was woven. The making of these talismans was supposedly taught to the Ojibwe by Asibikaashi, a Spider Woman, and they were hung from children's cradleboards to act as

Kundika (water sprinkler), 1150–1200 CE, celadon-glazed, thrown stoneware with inlaid decoration, 35.5 cm high.

Tombstones with urn-and-willow motif, all 1790s. Granary and King's Chapel cemeteries, Boston, Massachusetts.

a kind of dream sieve, catching the bad dreams and letting the good ones through.[28]

Because demon-repelling powers were attributed to the willow in China, branches were bound into whisks used to sweep ancestors' tombs during the annual Qingming festival or placed on them to ward off evil spirits, and celebrants wore willow wreaths or twigs.[29] Unsurprisingly, given its widely perceived link with the dead and with mourning, willow has played a significant role in the funerary rites and paraphernalia of cultures around the world. Arrowheads in the shape of willow leaves have been found in Stone Age burials, and willow-leaf crowns and garlands adorned mummies in ancient Egyptian tombs.[30] The role of willow in mourning could be extremely visceral: on a day of burial, young males of the Omaha would make parallel incisions in their forearms and, 'lifting the skin between these gashes', thrust in 'the stems of willow twigs'. The blood which ran down the twigs, like the mourners' tears, was a sign of sympathy for the bereaved.[31] In other times and places, willow's role was more impersonal. Towards the close of the eighteenth century, depictions of willows and urns became a popular design for gravestones in New England and were widespread by the Victorian period. If the occasional urn is inscribed with the name of the dead, most of them are blank, serving as anonymous and universal figures above the names and dates.[32] British mourning jewellery from the same period often employs the willow-and-urn motif, but personalizes it through inscriptions and sometimes the inclusion of the hair of the deceased.

The willows on tombstones and pins are signs of grief and symbols of the afterlife. The willow's association with death, however, was not always so benign. If the Chinese believed its virtues could assist in exorcisms,[33] in Europe the willow was commonly thought to be one of the trees on which Judas hanged himself, and popular superstition held that it was 'planted by the devil in order to lure people to suicide by the peculiar restful swinging of its branches'.[34] Ghosts could be driven out of houses and wedged into willows, and it was widely believed that spectres and poltergeists were condemned to live inside hollow trees, especially willows. In some places removing the bark of trees was assumed to damage the spirits that live inside them. The punishments meted out by Old German law for 'forest sacrileges' were grim: anyone who peeled a willow would be disembowelled and his or her entrails used to wrap the stripped trunk.[35] A curious, pseudo-scientific use for willows proposed by the German botanist Johann Friedrich Gmelin in the eighteenth century was perhaps influenced by the idea that willows could contain malevolent spirits: he advised planting them between cemeteries and towns so that they could 'absorb the mephitic vapours that escape from the graves'.[36]

The darker side of willow is suggested by the close link between the words witch, wicca, wicked and wicker. The word wicked derives from the old English *wicca* or wizard, the female version of which is *wiccian*, witch. Although wicker comes from the Danish *vigger*, meaning willow, it is also connected with the verb *viker*, to bend, the old English version of which is *wican*, to give way.[37] The suppleness of willow becomes, through this connection, a dangerous and potentially demonic quality. Superstitions and folk tales reflect the deep roots of this association of willow and witchery. Willows were believed to be both the 'meeting place and abiding place of witches'; a German proverb warns,

if you shall be tramping a desolate country alone between
the middle of the night and the break of day, and shall hear
a voice luring or laughing from a thicket of willows, beware,
for it is Kundry, the witch of 'Parsifal', who is there.[38]

Willow, the 'witches' tree', has been used in broomsticks and is the supposed source of witches' feline familiars, through transformation of the
cat-kins of *pussy* willows (this linguistic connection is found in many
European languages: catkins are *chatons* in French and *Kätzchen* in German).

It is no coincidence that one of the most famous (fictional)
witches of the twentieth century, Buffy the Vampire Slayer's best friend,
is named Willow. Her magical studies are repeatedly described as
'budding', and the character, like her vegetable namesake, is involved
in a continual process of becoming and hybridization: Willow Rosenberg,
who exhibits the most flexible character in the show, is Jewish and
pagan, heterosexual and lesbian, innocent and monstrous, necromancer
and goddess of life. Her destructive foray into dark magic is necessary
for her eventual transformation into the radiant white Willow. Her
character's ethics, corporeality and identity are more fluid than any
other's in the show; it is because she experiences first-hand the 'life *in*
death' and 'monstrosity *in* humanity' that she alone can save the world.[39]

Mourning pin, 1787,
enamelled gold, ivory and
watercolour under glass,
2.8 x 1.7 x 0.6 cm.

If witches are both frightening and potentially nurturing, so are other willowy women, as folktales from East to West attest. In one Japanese legend, a single father brings his baby daughter to a willow, whereupon a beautiful woman – the human incarnation of the tree – appears and breastfeeds the child. When the child grows up and finds she herself cannot breastfeed, she brings her own baby to the willow for sustenance.[40] A Czech story tells of a willow nymph who married a mortal and bore him a child. They lived happily until he chopped down her willow tree, whereupon she instantly died. He made a cradle out of the wood which calmed the baby and, when the child was old enough, it conversed with its dead mother through a willow pipe made from twigs growing on the stump of its mother's erstwhile home.[41] The Yuma or Quechan from the southwestern United States have a legend that the sun made two willow flutes out of the trees that grew in the water where she (the sun) was bathing. She gave birth to twins who, as adults, played the flutes to seduce women.[42]

Willow is renowned as a musical tree. Wind and string instruments have been created from willow for at least a millennium, though they have not always produced sounds as euphonious as the wind whispering through the tree's leaves. A case in point is the English 'whit-horn'. Until the mid-nineteenth century, a number of villages in Oxfordshire celebrated the 'Whit Hunt' on Whit Monday (Whitsun or Pentecost is the seventh Sunday after Easter), when the inhabitants were allowed to kill and eat a stag. The hunt was announced by the blowing of whit-horns or 'peeling-horns', funnel-shaped instruments made of a long, spiralling strip of willow bark pinned together with thorns and fitted with a willow bark reed at the narrow end.[43] Similar bark horns played a part in Whitsun celebrations in France and Croatia, where they were blown at the head of processions, and in Switzerland.[44] Henry Balfour, the first curator of Oxford University's Pitt Rivers Museum, collected several specimens of the English whit-horn and described them as less 'instruments of music' than of 'noise'.[45]

More melodious willow flutes, often played by shepherds, also figured in Whitsun festivals in Bohemia and May festivals in France.[46]

Whit-horn from Witney, Oxfordshire, *c.* 1890s.

The most sophisticated music produced on a woodwind willow instrument, however, is Scandinavian in origin. The willow or sallow flute (*seljefløyte* in Norwegian, *sälgflöjt* in Swedish) was traditionally played by herders in the spring and early summer. Historically, this simple instrument was made of a length of freshly cut willow from which the bark had been removed in one piece to create a long, hollow tube; the shaft was cut on one side near the top to create a mouthpiece and had no finger holes. Such flutes work only for a few weeks, until the bark dries out and splits. Played by blowing over the mouthpiece with varying degrees of intensity and by covering or uncovering the end of the flute, the *seljefløyte* produces high, breathy sounds in the overtone register that can resemble birdsong. It remains an important folk instrument in Scandinavia, though most contemporary 'willow flutes' are made of plastic (wrapped in birch bark to seem more natural).[47]

By far the most sophisticated willow instrument is the early Irish or Gaelic harp (*cláirseach* in Irish, *clàrsach* in Scots), its silhouette now instantly recognizable from the Guinness beer trademark. The *clàrsach* is a wire-stringed instrument with a single, hollowed-out piece of willow for the soundbox. Compared to the willow flute's almost eerie wildness, the early Irish harp's music is melancholy, somewhat austere and courtly, and willow is key to its rich if sombre sound. The metal strings must be held in tension by a hardwood, and willow, a tough but relatively soft and pliable hardwood, smooths the sound of the plucked strings, which would, with another material, sound brighter and more

Patrick Quin; Harper to the Irish Harp Society, engraving after a painting by Eliza Trotter, 1905.

pingy. The result is a lush, mellow sustain that supports the melody and the singer whom the harp historically accompanied.

The *clàrsach* was played by highly trained court harpers in Ireland and the Scottish highlands in the medieval period, usually as an accom - paniment to poetry recitations. These musicians travelled further afield during the Renaissance (Elizabeth 1 employed an Irish harper) and further still when the aristocratic system could no longer afford to maintain court musicians: itinerant harpers played throughout Europe in the sixteenth and seventeenth centuries. A Romantic portrait of the late eighteenth-century harper Patrick Quin shows the musician seated on a mossy stone at the side of a river, under the shade of a venerable tree, playing the Otway harp, which is dated between the sixteenth and eighteenth centuries and is now in the collection of Trinity College Dublin. The portrait – of the harp as well as the harper – has an appropriately elegiac tone, as by the early nineteenth century the early Irish harp had fallen into almost complete disuse (an instrument called the Irish or Gaelic harp invented in the nineteenth century differs significantly from the earlier instrument), and has only been revived in recent decades through the creation of replicas of extant examples in museum collections.[48]

The early Irish harp was linked, at various times, with resistance to English rule. Willow has in other ways played a significant role in politics, not always a purely symbolic one. As a political material, willow is capable of binding and parting, and representing both justice and tyranny. Various Native American groups sealed treaties with the cere - monial sharing of a *calumet*, or peace pipe, in which the bark of the red willow was commonly smoked, along with other plant substances including dried and powdered willow leaves.[49] Willow also served as a binding seal and symbol of authority in other legalistic settings: from the twelfth to the fifteenth centuries, a peeled willow wand served as the 'rod of justice' for the rulers of the Scottish isles, known as the Lords of the Isles, and was held when pronouncing justice.[50]

In China, the willow was often used as an image of benevolent rule. In the *Shi Jing*, a book of ancient odes dating from the tenth to seventh centuries BCE, the 'luxuriant willow tree' under whose shade one would like to rest was used as a metaphor for good kingship,[51] and due to its prominence in royal gardens and parks, it was some-times called the 'imperial willow' or the 'mandarin willow'.[52] When the Manchus conquered China in 1644 and brought an end to Ming rule, they used willow in a practical as well as symbolic way, and on an unparalleled scale, to cement the authority of the Qing dynasty. They built the 'willow palisade' (*liutiaobian*) in northeast China, a vegetal wall over 1,000 kilometres long and a botanical rival to the Great Wall.

The Manchus were an ethnic minority, yet after an initial period of resistance they established a rule of unprecedented economic expansion and prosperity, and acquired vast territories for the empire including Mongolia and Tibet. The Manchu rulers adopted some Han Chinese customs, made alliances with Mongol princes and bureaucratically unified the empire, but they were also keen to preserve their distinct martial and nomadic steppe identity. Thus, from 1644 to the 1680s they constructed internal barriers of ditches and embankments planted with willows, the branches of one tree tied to the next to create a continuous hedge. The palisade was punctuated at regular intervals with guarded gates and served to separate the realms in which the Mongols, the Manchus and a mixture of Manchu and Han lived. Although it was maintained for over two centuries, the willow wall functioned more as a psychological than a physical deterrent, one rendered gradually unnecessary by growth and cultural integration.[53]

Gong Xian, an exiled Ming loyalist painter and poet in the early years of the Qing dynasty, identified not with the graceful weeping willow or other cultivated varieties, but with wild, stunted, uncared-for willows of no particular species, which he adopted as a symbol of his exile. In a series of mid-seventeenth-century willow paintings

Detail of the willow palisade on a map of China from Rigobert Bonne, *Atlas de toutes les parties connues du globe terrestre* (Geneva, 1780). One can see the west and east sections of the palisade, indicated as lines sprouting little trees, screening off the Liaodong peninsula, and a northern segment separating Mongol and Manchurian lands.

Pierre-Jean-Joseph-Denis Crussaire, *The Mysterious Urn, c.* 1793, etching and stipple.

and poems, marshland willows, whose primary characteristics are their neglect and struggle to survive, serve as a symbol of his grief, harsh lifestyle and resistance. He likened himself and others exiled by, in his view, an illegitimate Manchu ruler to abandoned willows 'forced to live the plain lives of commoners, exposed to the shifting winds of fate and cast beyond the pale of human activity.'[54] The 'pale' in this case was quite literally the willow palisade, its willows cultivated by the

The Political Weeping Willow, 1791, hand-coloured etching.

empire to exclude him. The benign rule of the fourth Qing emperor, Kangxi, though, 'went far to soften the identity of the tree with imposed or foreign domination', and during his reign the image of the weeping willow became popular again in the arts.[55]

Willows are frequently pollarded. The word pollard comes from the early modern Dutch *pol*, meaning top or head. The modern meanings of the verb 'to poll' include to count heads, to vote, to behead and to remove the top branches of trees. The perhaps unexpected association of the pollard with democracy and decapitation may evoke the French Revolution. Intriguingly, in a number of Revolutionary-period prints mourning the family of Louis XVI, the majestic weeping willow appears as a symbol of grief, one irreparably marked by its pollarded other. *The Mysterious Urn* from c. 1793 at first appears to be a generic mourning image featuring an incense-wafting urn and a willow. On closer inspection, however, silhouettes become visible both in the foliage of the tree and in the outlines of the urn itself: profiles of Louis

XVI and Marie Antoinette appear as negative images on either side of the urn, while their children's heads hang in the tree, whose foliage comes to read as both hair and dripping blood.[56] The grief-stricken female figure represents France, and the willow both memorializes and renders visible the absence of her head(s).

The British response to the French Revolution was mixed. The radical Whig politician Charles James Fox, for example, supported the revolutionaries; his friend and fellow Whig Edmund Burke did not. Their quarrel reached its apogee in Parliament on 6 May 1791 when Burke became so angry that he crossed the floor to sit with the Tories and Fox broke down and wept.[57] A satirical print published a week later shows Fox as a weeping willow, tears cascading past his white cravat and pooling at his feet, his arms stretched wide in a Christ-like pose mocking his betrayal by Burke, his Judas.

While it may seem far removed from both pagan rites and political dramas, cricket is another arena in which willow encompasses ideological poles and serves a ritual purpose. The cricket bat, often referred to simply as 'the willow', is painstakingly crafted out of wedges of *S. alba*. Segments of trunk are cut into clefts so the grain of the wood runs parallel to the front of the bat, which is then shaped and pressed.[58] Today only a handful of skilled makers craft cricket bats out of white willow the traditional way, but their expensive 'willows' are the professional players' choice.

Historically, cricket has functioned as a sport in which class, race and ethnic struggles have been both expressed and sublimated. In the Victorian period, on cricket pitches from the West Indies to Singa-pore, 'class and racial divisions between Gentlemen and Players and Natives and Masters were supposed to be batted away with willow and leather'.[59] Despite British colonizers' doubts about the ability of natives to learn cricket and thus the sport's potential efficacy in the 'civilizing process', it was taken up with passion. In Tonga (a British protectorate until 1970), for example, it became so popular that the government had to limit the days of the week on which it could be played, as the populace 'sacrificed nearly all their time' to it, often playing 60-a-side in games that lasted for weeks.[60] They became, as various colonial reports indicate, 'first-rate cricketers', playing 'an eleven of every man-of-war' that visited the islands.[61] The British explorer Hugh Hastings Romilly summed up the situation nicely: 'We came there professing to teach them the game, but I am afraid to say by how much we were defeated.'[62]

It has been argued that the 'imperial game' was 'really about the colonial quest for identity in the face of the colonizers' search for authority'.[63] Each side changed the other, and willow-wielding colonial subjects transformed the history, style and significance of the game. The 'innovative batting style' of Ranjitsinhji, prince of Nawanagar and player for England, helped popularize 'the leg glance', for example.[64] The Trobriand Islanders changed the rules, implements and ritual purpose of the game entirely to suit their needs. In the Pacific islands, the Tongan way of playing was so popular that other peoples, such as the Samoans, played cricket *faʻa Tonga*, or Tonga style.[65] A photograph from the 1880s shows Tongan cricketers dressed not in cricket whites but in hybrid attire: Western shirts paired with the traditional *tupenu* (a sarong-like skirt). The same hybridity informs the sport today, which is no longer so white in multiple senses: the uniform white faces, white attire and white bats of traditional English cricket have given way to cricketers of diverse heritages, brightly coloured uniforms and willow bats adorned with polychrome or black graphics.

We will wind up this chapter by considering a practice in which mythic, magic, religious and political concerns have become, in its long reception history, thoroughly intertwined: the creation of wicker men. Accounts of Druidic human sacrifice in wicker men are traceable to Julius Caesar's *Commentaries on the Gallic War*, written in the 50s BCE, in which he mentions 'state' sacrifices made by the Gallic people to propitiate the gods. These rites, orchestrated by the Druids, involved 'colossal images, the limbs of which, made of wickerwork, they fill[ed] with living men and set on fire; and the victims perish[ed], encompassed by the flames'.[66] Criminals were the victims of choice, though innocents were used if no murderers and thieves were available, or to supplement

Tongan cricket team, 1880s.

their numbers. No archaeological evidence has been found to confirm this report of vast willow immolation structures (although the Druids did practise human sacrifice). Historians have speculated that this ritual was invented by Caesar to serve his rhetorical aim of justifying the Gallic wars (by suggesting that the barbaric, human-sacrificing Gauls and Britons were in dire need of Roman civilizing).[67]

Strabo, Diodorus and other ancient writers repeated Caesar's story, but the practice was neither illustrated nor subject to analysis until 1676, when the English antiquary Aylett Sammes published his *Britannia Antiqua Illustrata; or, The Antiquities of Ancient Britain*. Sammes introduced the topic by more or less quoting Caesar's description of the rite, adding a few comments on construction (the limbs are 'weaved together in the nature of Basket-ware') and the pathos of the sacrifice ('and so destroy'd the poor Creatures in the Smoak and flames'). How - ever, thinking it 'not amiss to represent the view' given 'the strange - ness of [the] Custome', he included an engraving which became the subsequent model for all representations of such wicker figures. Sammes felt certain that such an unusual rite had to be motivated by some historical event, presumably one of 'great occasion', and he speculated that the 'Magnitude of the Statue itself' might be a clue to its origin. He believed that the Phoenicians, a race of relative giants compared to the Britons and Gauls, had invaded and enslaved them in antiquity. Perhaps 'publick detestation of that Slavery they once endured' led to the introduction of 'this vast figure of a Man, made up in *Wicker* or *Osyer* work ... in scorn and derision of [the Phoenicians], having now lost their power over them, although the cause why they were first made (as it often falls out) might be forgotten, and so the Representation only remain'.[68] This unique psychological explanation of the Druids' wicker men determined the character of Sammes's engraving. The author was, as the historian Ronald Hutton puts it, something of 'an apologist for Druids',[69] and his illustration, while a product of fantasy, is considerably less sensationalist than later ones.

The figure represented by the willow 'image' is a fair-haired, well-groomed character looking stoically into the distance. The face and neck are represented naturalistically, and the rest of the body exhibits a geometrically regular construction, with each willow 'stake' running parallel to the next and bales of hay stacked neatly around each foot. There are hints of violence – in the struggling couple in the upper thigh and the smoke rising from the bottom left – but overall the image suggests order and restraint. The arrangement of the couple in the thigh even echoes the composition of Bernini's sculpted *Rape of the Sabines* and thus links this practice of the ancient Britons to an ancient Roman act of violence undertaken out of civic necessity. Foreground vegetation and rocks distance us spatially, as we are distanced temporally, from the scene, which we are encouraged to view dispassionately, or at least with an eye towards understanding the custom as the cultural artefact of an organized people rather than a barbaric practice to be condemned outright.

Later representations showed considerably less anthropological appreciation of the practice. Far from a celebration of emancipation from slavery, the ritual came to be understood as pure pagan

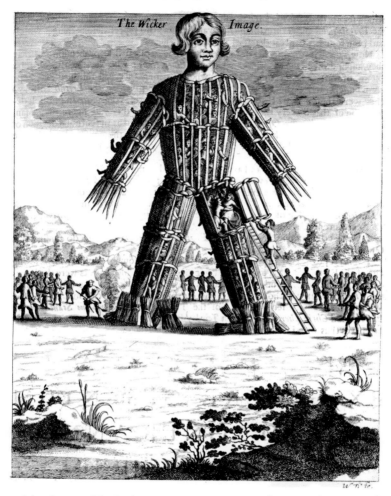

Aylett Sammes, 'The Wicker Image', in *Britannia Antiqua Illustrata; or, The Antiquities of Ancient Britain* (London, 1676).

wickedness. Robert Southey, the once radical Romantic poet who became a staunch conservative in his later years, discussed the ancient Britons in his history of the Church of 1824. He deemed their sexual mores as 'pernicious' as 'their idolatry', and in rites such as the Druids' burning of the wicker men he imagined 'naked women, stained with the dark blue dye of woad', assisting as the victims, guilty or innocent, were 'thrust in' the death trap.[70] An illustration published in the

Saturday Magazine in 1832 to accompany an excerpt from Southey attempts to capture the text's sense of immediacy.[71] The giant structure is pressed up close to the picture plane, forcing us to confront the faces of the multitude of victims crammed untidily into the wicker-work, while half-naked women in the foreground, one of whom cannot bear to look at the soon-to-be burnt offering, suggest the revulsion the viewer should feel (while providing some titillation – a more acceptable sort of fleshly offering). The construction of the wicker man is decidedly less plausible, and certainly shoddier, than in Sammes's version, and its blank-eyed, mask-like face and frontal pose suggest the 'primitive' state of its builders. Cloaked figures framing

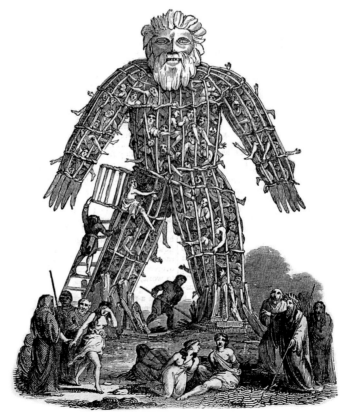

'Gigantic Druidical Idol', in 'Superstitions of the Druids', *Saturday Magazine* (1832).

the image at bottom left and right, and the shadows that encompass the bottom third of the illustration, assure the viewer that the scene takes place in pagan darkness.

The *Saturday Magazine* illustration was recycled in various forms in the 1830s and beyond in weekly magazines. Most of the articles it accompanied were sensationalist rather than anthropologically edifying; one in the French *Magasin pittoresque* queries the lack of evidence for the Druids' 'execrable use of human holocausts', only to conclude that, while one would like to discount such tales of horror, 'the recent cruelties of the inquisition' are sufficient proof of the 'crimes of which the human species are guilty'.[72] British missionary magazines aimed at children also reproduced variants of the image – frighteningly gory scenes in dramatic *chiaroscuro* (*sans* naked ladies, of course).[73] Depraved Druidic basketware then largely disappeared from visual culture until the film *The Wicker Man* of 1973, now a cult classic, revived it for the popular imagination.

The film presents itself as an anthropological documentary and follows the investigation of Sergeant Howie, a strait-laced West Highland Constabulary officer, into the possible disappearance of a twelve-year-old girl from Summerisle. As Howie explores the community, he witnesses lascivious pagan celebrations and finds himself tempted by the comely innkeeper's daughter, Willow. He learns that the island's crops have failed, and he comes to suspect that at the upcoming May Day festival the missing girl will be sacrificed. The islanders, however, have lured the sergeant there for that purpose, and at the climax of the film they strip him, wash his hands, dress him in white robes and anoint him before locking him inside the wicker man. The gigantic effigy (see overleaf), filled with animals as well as Sergeant Howie, is set alight, while the islanders dance and sing around their sacrifice and the martyr prays to his god. The film is remarkably restrained, its horror revealed only at the end with the vision of the wicker man to which the whole narrative has slowly and inexorably led.

The popularity of *The Wicker Man* has inspired an American remake and a sequel (*The Wicker Tree*, 2012). It has also spawned the Wickerman

Burning of the wicker man, film still from *The Wicker Man* (1973).

Festival, an annual Scottish alternative music event, which concludes each year with the burning of a giant willow effigy. The artists Alex Rigg and Trevor Leat made the festival's sculpture in 2011. A humanoid body topped with a stag's head, the 15-m sculpture references elements of the original film – the animal masks worn by the participants in the May Day festival as well as the wicker man itself – while also suggesting other mythical expiations such as the metamorphosis of Actaeon, who was punished for spying on the goddess Diana bathing. The fascination with such immolations perhaps led to the burning of Serena de la Hey's *Willow Man*, a 12-m figure in black maul willow erected in 2001 beside the M5 in Somerset to personify the local willow industry (it was subsequently rebuilt).

Although Druidic wicker men hold a privileged place in the popular imagination, there is a broader European tradition of making and burning willow effigies in association with both Christian and pagan celebrations. On Midsummer's Eve, the summer solstice, the burning of *mannequins d'osier* (wicker figures) was common in France before the nineteenth century. Like the Midsummer bonfires lit elsewhere, such burnings were meant to drive away evil spirits. Other occasions were

Alex Rigg and Trevor Leat, *Wickerman*, 2011, willow over steel armature, 15 m high.

sometimes marked by a similar rite: in Paris a willow effigy called 'le géant de la rue aux Ours' was burned every year on 3 July until 1643, supposedly to commemorate the burning of a blasphemous soldier in 1418. Mannhardt, however, deems this a fable concocted to explain the regional deviation of the parish of Ours from the more widespread practice of burning the willow mannequin on Midsummer's Eve.[74] In Scotland, Hogmanay (the Scots word for the last day of the year) is celebrated with the burning of a wicker effigy on 29 December, while in Ireland, Beltane, or May Day, the beginning of summer, was cele- brated with bonfires. Although effigies were not traditionally burnt, folk etymology derives Beltane from 'the fires of Bel', a Sumerian sun god who supplanted Belili, the goddess of willows, the moon, the under- world, and waters, known as the 'Willow Mother';[75] Beltane burnings are thus, figuratively, willow immolations.

Not all willow effigies were burnt, however. From the fifteenth to the early seventeenth centuries, the funerary rites of French kings incorporated willow mannequins. When a monarch died, wax sculp- tures of his hands and face were attached to a wicker body 'like the dummies at a costumier's' and dressed in finery.[76] This effigy was then exhibited in state and played an important role in the funerary rites. During the medieval period and into the Renaissance, the liv- ing king was perceived to have two bodies: a natural, earthly one and a spiritual one emblematic of his divinely ordained kingship. After the king's death, these two bodies separated; the mortal remains were consigned to a coffin while the wicker effigy continued to manifest 'the royal Majesty' until the coronation of the new king. As a manifes- tation of royal authority, the effigy was treated as a living king (during the funerary rites of Francis I it was served with elaborate meals).[77] Only a vegetable body was capable of sustaining the paradox, 'The king is dead. Long live the king!'

In some places gigantic willow effigies have played, and still play, an important role in civic life. In many French and Belgian towns they actually walk the streets. Every year since 1550 the town of Dunkerque, for example, has celebrated the coming of spring with a carnival in

Louis Watteau, *La famille du grand gayant de Douai*, 1780, oil on wood, 67 x 92 cm.

which a willow giant is paraded. The *Reuze* (Flemish for giant) represents a Scandinavian warrior named Allowyn who was converted to Christianity by the town's patron saint and who then fortified the town. Supposedly every Flemish town once had one or more giants,[78] usually mythic founders or defenders, though some were created to commemorate specific events. Douai celebrates a historic victory over the French in 1479 (when it was still part of Flemish territory) on the Sunday closest to 7 July with a festival, first held in 1480, called 'Le Gayant' (the giant). It involves a family of enormous wicker mannequins – Gayant, his wife and their three children – parading through the city. The willow frames of the mannequins support sculpted and painted heads, movable arms and elaborate costumes. Although the mannequins have been rebuilt many times, one Gayant's head is said to have been painted by Rubens.[79] Today's mannequins, built in the post-war period, sport historical costumes, but in the past the giants wore more contemporary garb: a painting of 1780 shows the willow creatures in stylish eighteenth-century attire. Perhaps these chic costumes reflect the contemporary use of *mannequins d'osier* as dressmakers' forms. Wickerwork dummies for tailoring first came into use around 1750, and were made to order according to the patron's measurements; the fashion icon Madame de Pompadour had one.[80] Willow mannequins later gave way to stuffed models, perhaps in part because these wicker doubles too strongly evoked pagan beliefs and practices.

Anatole France's novel *Le Mannequin d'osier* (1898) certainly suggests that undercurrents of myth, dark magic and human sacrifice lurk within the fashionable commodity of the dressmaker's dummy. The story revolves around M. Bergeret, a mediocre professor of philology in a provincial town. His marital relations are a constant vexation: Mme Bergeret regards herself as superior to him and insists on keeping her *mannequin d'osier* in his tiny, cramped study. After he catches her in flagrante with his favourite student, he retreats to his scholarly lair only to see the mannequin. Wicker chicken coops and sacrifices of slaves in willow effigies flash through his mind, and the mannequin 'becomes' the grotesque, hated Mme Bergeret herself, emblematic of his perceived castration, captivity and martyrdom. In a fit of rage, he throws himself upon the wicker torso, clasps it, 'cracks the willow of the bodice like the cartilage of ribs', stamps on it and carries it 'groaning and mutilated' to the window, where he throws it out into the neighbouring cooper's yard. After this outburst, M. Bergeret ignores his wife so totally that she feels she no longer counts as 'a person, or even a thing'. The neighbour returns the mannequin to Mme Bergeret, and she keeps the wounded figure suggestive of black magic – a commodity fetish turned life-size voodoo doll – in the conjugal chamber from which M. Bergeret has departed, where it functions as a mirror in which she witnesses her own slow death. In the end, M. Bergeret gleefully succeeds in driving her from the house.[81] Willow wares in France's novel blur the line between persons and things. As we will see in the next chapter, this suggestion of a symbiotic relationship is characteristic more broadly of how humans have shaped, and been shaped by, their willowy creations.

two

Willowy Forms

❦

Throughout history, willow has furnished materials for objects
and structures essential to human culture, including arrows,
baskets, bee skeps, brooms, coffins, cooking pots, coracles,
cradles, fish traps, fences, furniture, huts, ladders, lattices, musical instruments, nets, trunks, wattle walls and winnowing trays. This chapter will
examine some of the useful, playful and often very beautiful objects
produced from willow, as well as some of the more fantastic willow con -
structions designed for communal habitation and aesthetic experience.

One of the oldest textiles discovered to date is a fishing net made
of willow bast (the inner bark) from the eighth or ninth millennium
BCE. It was found in Finland, and similar nets from the fifth millennium have been unearthed in Denmark.[1] Ancient remains of various
willow wares, from Native American nets and water bottles to Meso-
potamian coffins, attest to the importance of *Salix* for both survival
and symbolic rites. We will begin our study of the material culture of
willow with basket-making, probably the earliest and most widespread craft, one critical for the shift from hunter-gatherer to farming and pastoralist groups and thus to the development of human
culture and civilization.

Basketry lies somewhere between the textile arts and architecture.
Akin to other natural art forms like birds' nests and honeycombs,
baskets are made to suit their environments and purposes, but their
creators have also developed a seemingly infinite variety of forms
and patterns in response to a multitude of functions and aesthetic

predilections. In former centuries basketry was imbricated in virtu-ally every aspect of daily life and death (the word coffin comes from the old French *cofin*, meaning little basket). Baskets accompanied our pleasures and grief, work and play. Yet despite something of a revival in recent decades as a craft and form of art, basketry has largely disappeared from our consciousness, as handmade containers and carriers have been replaced, in much of the world, by mass-produced plastic counterparts.

Willow's suppleness makes it one of the most valued basketry materials; as one appreciator put it, the '"note" of the willow is pliancy, and the very name, connected, it is said, etymologically with "willing," emphasizes the quality that makes it so valuable to the basket-weaver'.[2] Capitalizing on willow's 'kindness', the basket-maker can create con-tainers of great elegance and strength – and which imbue everyday activities with poetry. In her memoir *Isvor: The Country of Willows*, Princess Marthe Bibesco described with longing the 'green cone-shaped baskets, made of the plaited twigs of willow saplings, and lined inside with fresh leaves' used by Romanian peasants to carry raspberries down from the hills,[3] and virtually every culture in the northern hemisphere has made willow baskets whose forms, colours, smells and uses evoke landscapes, seasons, tastes and other memories.

Native Americans have long used willow to make burden baskets, gathering baskets, seedbeaters, hats and cradles. They have ground acorns in mortar hoppers (bottomless baskets placed on a stone against which the nuts are smashed), roasted pinenuts by flipping them with hot coals in winnowing baskets, and made soup in cooking baskets. Water bottles made of tightly twined or coiled, pitch-covered willow allowed freedom of movement and the settling of desert areas.[4] In the Great Basin area in the western United States, which has one of the richest willow basketry traditions, makers at first wove with whole shoots of willow, gradually refining their techniques and incorporating split and peeled wands into their works,[5] and dyeing or 'sunburning' the willow (sunlight turns the inner bark a rusty brown colour) to allow the creation of patterns. Other plant materials, feathers, shells and beads were also

Paiute water bottle, *c.* 1900, willow and piñon pitch, 10.8 × 17.8 cm.

sometimes incorporated to create visually rich containers, some of which had semi-sacred uses.

Willow was and remains a common foundation material for Native baskets. Coiling, one of the major basketry techniques of the American West, is predominantly used to create circular and oval forms. Foundation rods spiral upwards from the centre of the basket's base to its top rim; these are sewn together with wefts, often so tightly that the vessel can hold liquids. By substituting different weft materials or adding a weft overlay (a kind of embroidery), makers can introduce patterns and figures into the very structure of the coiled form. The spread of coiled basketry has been deemed the 'greatest single artistic movement in Native California art history',[6] and today in art galleries as well as ethnographic or anthropological collections its forms and patterns are appreciated at least as much for their aesthetic as for their use value.

The Pomo of central California are renowned for their feather-covered willow 'fancy' or 'treasure' baskets, which were often passed down as family heirlooms and are much coveted by collectors. The

Pomo basket, *c.* 1890–1910, willow, clamshell discs, red woodpecker feathers, quail
topknots and other plant materials, 17.8 cm diameter.

Pomo also produced more utilitarian objects using a variety of *Salix*
species and different parts (the long, thin roots for fine work, the
larger limbs for weirs, and so on).[7] They developed basket types for
seemingly every stage of life as well as every need; babies, for example,
were carried and bathed in willow baskets. A particularly exquisite late
nineteenth- or early twentieth-century treasure basket is decorated with
black quail topknots, red woodpecker feathers, clamshell discs, glass
beads and black stitched bracken fern or sedge patterns. The materials
alone attest to the maker's or makers' investment in the object: grind-
ing and polishing the shells and finding the right feathers would
have taken a great deal of time and labour. This small basket has a
low, rotund body and a wide mouth; its snug but accommodating
shape evokes both nests and gourds, and the range of its materials –
from plants and creatures native to earth, water and sky – marks it as
a suitable container for any of the world's treasures, indeed, makes it a
little world unto itself.

While native basketry is strongly linked with traditional forms
and patterns, there is an equally vibrant history of innovation and
response to cross-cultural encounters and new markets. The works of

the legendary Washoe artist Louisa Keyser (*c.* 1829–1925) are a case in point. Keyser's Washoe name was Dabuda, meaning young willow, and as a child she learned to make coiled willow baskets. Starting in 1895, she sold her work exclusively through Cohn Emporium in Carson City, Nevada, and in response to the rising demand for Native American basketry, avidly collected by museums and connoisseurs, she invented a new basket form, the *degíkup*, designed for aesthetic appeal alone. The sides of these vessels gently swell out from a narrow base, reaching their maximum width three-quarters of the way up, then curve inward to a relatively small top opening, forming an almost heart-shaped vase. Keyser usually worked with a three-rod willow foundation for her coiled baskets, and spliced bracken fern and redbud into the willow threads to create black and red patterns on the golden ground of the willow.

A *degíkup* from *c.* 1918 exemplifies the sophisticated yet organic relation of sculptural form and surface decoration in Keyser's work. Beginning just above the base, four groups of three decorative 'columns'

Louisa Keyser (Dat So La Lee), *Degíkup, c.* 1918, willow, bracken fern and redbud, 24.8 × 36.8 cm.

composed of alternating red and black stepped pyramid shapes, from which tall isosceles triangles flare upward like flames or claws, are arrayed around the basket. As though in response to the curved form, the pyramids increase in size as the basket swells to its maximum diameter and shrink again towards the top. The centre column of each set of three rises vertically, while its flanking pair bow gently outwards, again stressing the robust form of the basket. The decoration is thus literally and figuratively integrated into the form of the basket; with minimal means and simple geometries, the *degíkup* simultaneously suggests purity and plenitude, stability and dynamism. It has been dubbed a masterwork and a national treasure,[8] and Keyser's baskets are some of the most sought after in the world. Fittingly in later life

Peasants carrying willow twigs for wicker baskets, first half of third century CE, mosaic from Saint Romain-en-Fal, France.

'Vannerie' in Denis Diderot, ed., *Encyclopédie; ou, Dictionnaire raisonné des sciences, des arts, et des metiers, Recueil des Planches sur les science et les arts libéraux* (Paris, 1772).

she changed her Washoe name to Dat So La Lee, meaning Queen of Washoe Basketmakers.

Europe has an equally long-standing and vibrant history of basket-making. A Roman mosaic from the third century CE shows a basket-maker in the midst of weaving a round-bottomed basket welcoming a delivery of willow rods. In the Roman world baskets were used for storage and transport, for containers ranging from perfume-bottle holders to farm carts. As in North America, water bottles were an important product; Pliny mentions that with stripped willow one can weave bottles 'more capacious than any that can be made of leather'.[9] Manuscript illuminations and woodcuts from the medieval and early modern periods depict a wide variety of baskets for domestic and agricultural use, as well as willow fencing. Basket-makers' guilds were formed in various European cities from the fourteenth to the sixteenth centuries,[10] and by the eighteenth century the basketry industries in many countries were highly developed and divided into specialities. An eighteenth-century engraving of a French workshop

Man's hat, 1810–20, woven skeined willow with silk ribbon and silk plain weave lining.

illustrates both the products and the process involved in basket-making: unstripped withies litter the foreground of the image, and at the far right a worker is engaged in splitting rods. At the left a weaver puts the finishing touches on the rim of a large basket, and pressed against the walls of the room is an assortment of willow wares: laundry and flower baskets, bird carriers, panniers and enormous transport baskets. At the centre three figures work on a ceremonial wicker sculp-ture of a soldier, and a child plays with a simple willow hoop. Three of the figures wear what may be willow hats; these were worn by men and women, and could be coarse or fine weave, casual or dressy.

In England, several types of willow have long been cultivated for basketry, including *Salix triandra* (almond-leaved willow), *S. purpurea* (purple or bitter willow) and *S. viminalis* (common osier). Once har-vested, willow withies are sorted by height and colour, then dried and stored. Fresh willow can be used directly for weaving, but dried rods must be soaked first to make them pliable. Some rods are left with their coloured bark intact, others peeled to reveal the white wood beneath. Others still are boiled with the bark on, which releases tannins that stain the inner wood; they are then peeled to produce rods of a red-brown colour. For centuries willow was peeled by pulling rods through 'brakes' made of cleft wood or metal; a nineteenth-century photograph shows a stand of brakes at which three women are peeling osiers (see overleaf). This process was made easier by the invention of boilers in the 1850s, and the need for hand-stripping was eliminated altogether in the 1930s, when machines capable of stripping whole bundles at a time were invented.

There are many basket-making techniques, but two commonly employed with willow in Britain and Europe are stake-and-strand and plaiting. Three traditional willow baskets by contemporary makers exhibit these techniques. At the top, Katherine Lewis's oval fitched

Kate Lynch, *The Whitening Season: Brian Lock and Brian White Drying Stripped Whites*, 2003, oil on paper.

Peeling osiers in Norfolk, 1888.

shopping basket is made of stakes twined together with thinner strands of willow twisting between them (the fitching). The simple orthogonals of the openwork base and sides are softened by the graceful curve of the rim, which is subtly accented with browner willow rods. In the centre, Adrian Charlton's *périgourdin* is a type of openwork vegetable basket that originated in the Périgord region of France. In these baskets, stakes like bicycle spokes seem to be 'miraculously held together by a plait which starts in the base and spirals around four times before it forms the border', though in fact the stakes are woven into and out of the plait at each turn of the spiral.[11] The *périgourdin*'s simple yet mesmeric form evokes airy openness as well as the intimate interiority of the snail shell. At the bottom, David Drew's oval frame basket is a stake-and-strand work in which a split rod, its halves placed side by side, forms a central keel that rises above the rim at either end. Stakes, like lines of longitude, splay out between the keel and frame, composed of two whole willow rods. Thin willow strands are twined over and under the stakes, creating a beautiful, balanced form that evokes both barques and cradles.

Unstripped willow baskets, top to bottom: Katherine Lewis, oval fitched shopper, 2011, 33 × 60 × 32 cm; Adrian Charlton, périgourdin, 2012, 25 × 46 × 28 cm; David Drew, oval frame basket, 2011, 25 × 51 × 29 cm.

Joan Carrigan, *Willow Bark Twill Basket*, 2008, 16.5 × 22.8 × 10.2 cm; Lise Bech, *Little Cairn Kinney*, 2009, 32 × 37 cm.

Other contemporary basket-makers deliberately blur the line between craft and art by making sculptural, and sometimes non-functional, objects. Four examples by Scottish, Canadian, Irish and Danish basket-makers indicate some of the range of contemporary art basketry. Lise Bech's *Little Cairn Kinney* is a 'landscaped pod' inspired by the ruggedly flowing geography of the Scottish hillside. Treated as a sensuous sculptural form rather than a utilitarian container, the piece, which seems to shift and move as you look at it, foregrounds the suppleness of willow and uses biomorphic forms and the earthy colour of *S. fragilis Sanguina* 'Flanders Red' to evoke nature and its forces. Joan Carrigan's *Willow Bark Twill Basket* is made, as the title suggests, with the bark of the willow rather than its withies. Sliced into thin, ribbon-like strips, the bark is plaited together in a complex twill pattern to create a tight but textured surface. The exterior of the bark faces outwards on the vertical and horizontal strips, while its golden-brown, smooth inner side runs on the diagonals, creating a complex and lyrical pattern. The juxtaposition of rustic roughness and precious golden highlights reads as the basket's sophisticated weaving together of hard and soft, exterior and interior, nature and culture. Joe Hogan's *Blue Catkin Vase* makes us see a simple vessel form afresh through its surprising use of colour and materials. The lovely blue skin of *S. daphnoides* wands suggests moving waters, from which shoots of budding willow emerge: this is a vase with the water and the flowers on the outside. Anne Folehave's softly scaly willow cauldron is ornamented with folded bits of recycled bicycle tires, creating an environmentally friendly form that evokes different realms, not unlike the Pomo fancy basket with its decorative feathers and clamshell discs.

In addition to art basketry, high-end design has helped bring about a revival of interest in willow. In the 'production series' by the late Finnish artist Markku Kosonen, the pieces are not woven; instead, Kosonen assembled willow shoots of varying thicknesses and bright

Joe Hogan, *Blue Catkin Vase*, 2008, 24 × 30 cm; Anne Folehave, *Willow Basket with Rubber Scales*, 2005, willow and bicycle rubber tube, 29 × 50 cm.

Markku Kosonen, baskets from the production series, 1990s, willow.

colours (orange, red, purple, green) Tinkertoy fashion. This simple system is used to comment on traditional basketry techniques. The spiral basket just below right of centre, for example, almost literalizes the idea of coiling, but willow sticks are used to hold apart rather than stitch together the coils. Others, at the bottom right and top centre, refer to stake-and-strand weaving, but leave the side stakes stranded, as it were (really unstranded) around the edges. In an interview Kosonen remarked that unstripped willow is ready for 'a grand new transformation',[12] one for which his own work has helped pave the way.

These recent examples are mostly luxury items, but until the second half of the twentieth century beautiful willow basketry was a necessity. Perhaps surprisingly, basket-making was not incompatible with urbanization and industrialization; indeed, it was indispensable for both processes. Urbanization would not have been possible without the transport of food and goods from the country to the city in baskets, and by the mid-nineteenth century, standardized baskets, trunks and hampers were needed for railway transport and postal deliveries; the Royal Mail employed its own basket-makers to make willow hampers.[13] During the First World War, the need for transportation containers was so great that most of Somerset's willow crop went into transport baskets and shell cases for ammunition. Thousands of pigeons employed as messengers were also carried in specially designed willow baskets. Two from around 1914 – a backpack and a collapsible cage – suggest something of the variety of willow forms created as part of the war

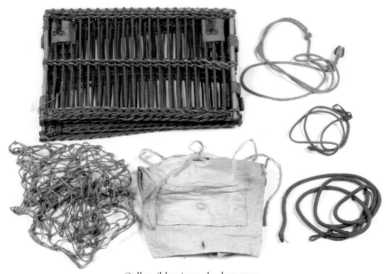

Collapsible pigeon basket, 1914.

Double pigeon
basket, 1914.

effort. In the Second World War, virtually the whole of Great Britain's
willow crop was used by the Ministry of Defence, particularly for air-
borne panniers which, thanks to willow's flexibility and strength,
could be filled with supplies and dropped from great heights without
breaking. Around two million were made before D-Day.[14]

Despite its homeliness and association with the pastoral tradition,
willow has in fact always been associated with war. One of the Greek
words for willow, ἰτέα, refers to shields or pikes made of willow as well
as to the plant itself, as shields in ancient Greece consisted of bronze
facing over a core of willow strips.[15] The Teutons similarly used woven
willow shields covered with buffalo hide.[16] The Japanese made bows
and arrows out of willow, and one possible etymology of *yanagi*, the
Japanese word for willow, is *ya no ki*, which means 'arrow tree' or the
tree from which arrows come.[17] Native American cultures also made
arrows and bows out of willow wands.[18] Gabions, or wickerwork
baskets filled with earth, functioned as protective fortifications, often

around gunners, from the medieval period onwards. And crack willow charcoal was used in gunpowder.

To return to willow baskets, however, they have an equally long-standing and vibrant history in the Far East. In China willow basketry has been used since at least the Zhou Dynasty (1046–256 BCE) for cooking, grain storage, transport and rice scoops.[19] There is evidence of Japanese willow basketry from the first century, and by the Edo period it was a thriving industry based in Toyooka. *S. koriyanagi* was woven into boxes that served as ceremonial gifts (*Yanagi-bako*) and light, strong, oblong baskets (*Yanagi-gori*) used for all kinds of storage and as travellers' trunks. With the latter, a slightly larger basket placed upside-down over the first served as a cover; one nineteenth-century travel guide highly recommended these as 'cheap, portable, capacious, and *contractible*'. Wrapped in oil paper and fastened with straps, they were a necessity for anyone who intended 'to rough it'.[20] Sturdier wicker trunks (*kori-kaban*) bound with leather bands became popular in the Meiji period (1868–1912).[21]

More than an accompaniment to travel, willow basketry has facilitated voyages over water and land, and even through the skies. Coracles, from the Welsh *cwrwgl*, are light, shallow, bowl-shaped boats made of a willow framework covered with hide or cloth coated with pitch. They have been used in Britain from pre-Roman times, and the Babylonians used similar willow boats, according to Herodotus.[22] The bodies of chariots, carts, coaches and prams have been made of woven willow, as have balloon baskets; some still are today. A wood engraving from 1875 shows a group of French balloonists in the 'Zenith', having reached an altitude of nearly 28,000 feet (see overleaf). Although two of the passengers have lost consciousness, they are safely contained by the wicker walls of their vessel. A drawing of the same ascent shows the balloonists observing a lunar halo and luminescent cross, offering an oneiric image of travelling to the moon, which rules the willow, in a basket!

The relative weightlessness and strength of willow has inspired fantasies of flight since the medieval period at least: Chaucer's

'The "Zenith" after reaching an altitude of nearly 28,000 feet', 1875,
wood engraving.

*Lunar Halo and Luminescent Cross Observed During the Balloon Zenith's Long Distance Flight from
Paris to Arcachon in March, 1875, c. 1875–80,* ink wash, lead white and graphite on paper.

Edward Burne-Jones, 'The House of Rumour', in *The Works of Geoffrey Chaucer* (Hammersmith, 1896).

unfinished *House of Fame*, written *c.* 1380, involves a giant flying willow basket. In book three of the narrator's journey he comes across a wicker edifice whirling 'swift as thought' above the ground. Made of yellow, green, red and white twigs woven into a form that is part-basket, part-cage, the house has as many entries as there are leaves on trees in summer and the roof is full of holes to let the sound fly out. Dropped through a window by an eagle, the narrator finds the house full of whisperings – all kinds of rumour, which spreads and expands with each retelling and finally, much altered, flies out through the apertures.[23] Edward Burne-Jones's illustration represents the airy willow vessel as a kind of flying Christmas pudding spinning through the landscape.

One of the most important early pioneers of actual rather than imaginary flight was indebted to willow. The German engineer Otto Lilienthal, who published *Birdflight as the Basis of Aviation* in 1889, designed and constructed a variety of gliders, achieving gliding flight in the 1890s. He and his brother Gustav had begun experiments

Wing-beat experiment, figure 19 in Otto Lilienthal, *Der Vogelflug als Grundlage der Fliegekunst* (1889).

in their teens; Gustav recalled that as children they were fascinated by the fable of the tired willow wren who is taught the principles of gliding by a kindly stork. In their earliest attempts, the brothers 'did not heed the lesson taught by our storks' – they began not by developing gliders to launch from a height, but by attempting to achieve lift-off through mechanically propelled wing-beating. One early contraption, like many of their later successful gilders, was made of willow rods and canvas coated with collodion, to make it as airtight as possible. Suspended and counterweighted, the brothers literally tried to climb into the sky (the machine functions rather like a StairMaster). Unsurprisingly, the 'requisite effort' was 'so great that we could maintain ourselves at a certain level only for a few seconds'. If the method was inexact, the materials were right: having tried other substances including feathers, the brothers found that 'round willow canes' were not only sufficiently light but also 'possessed the greatest resistance against breakage'.[24] Eventually they developed the *Normalsegelapparat*, or 'regular sailing apparatus'; a photograph from *c.* 1895 shows Otto conducting a gliding experiment with it. Having launched himself off a hill, the daring aeronaut dangles below the giant wings of his machine, its willow skeleton visible against the fabric. Otto, the 'glider king', made more than 2,000 gliding flights before a fatal crash on 9 August 1896.

If willow structures have facilitated aerial adventures, their earthbound counterparts have equally reflected their makers' flights of fancy. One of the most curious and imaginative speculations upon willow's architectural and community-building possibilities was concocted by Sir James Hall, a Scottish geologist. In a paper presented to the Royal Society of Edinburgh in 1797 and published the following year, Hall proposed that the forms of all Gothic architecture could be traced back to the construction techniques and material peculiarities of rustic edifices constructed out of willow. His motivation for publishing his theory – one which, he freely admitted, had no evidentiary

Lilienthal gliding experiment, *c.* 1895.

Willow rod nave with thatched roof, in Sir James Hall, 'On the Origin and Principles of Gothic Architecture', *Transactions of the Royal Society of Edinburgh*, 4 (1798), detail of plate III.

basis ('all direct testimony is wanting') – was dismay at his contemporaries' evaluation of classical Greek and Gothic architecture, the former celebrated for its rationality and beauty, the latter denigrated for its capricious and often gloomy character. Taking as his inspiration the ancient Roman architect Vitruvius' theory that the language of classical Greek architecture was based on timber prototypes, Hall proposed that stone Gothic architecture must likewise have a precedent in a different material that would rationally explain its construction system and ornament. While travelling through France in 1785, he observed peasants collecting willow wands, and it occurred to him that 'a rustic dwelling might be constructed of such rods, bearing a resemblance to works of Gothic architecture, and from which the peculiar forms of that style might have been derived'.[25] From the moment of this epiphany, he embarked on a research project that would occupy his spare time for the next forty years.

His work is, of necessity, a 'theoretical history' of Gothic architecture that purports to explain 'even the most intricate forms of this elaborate style' in terms of its 'simple origin'. He begins by imagining the willow construction of the basic forms of the cathedral: a nave with clustered pillars, a rib-vaulted roof and pointed arches. 'SUPPOSE', he instructs the reader, a 'set of round posts, driven firmly into the ground in two opposite rows', around each of which 'a set of long and flexible rods of willow' is rooted, clustered and tied near the ground and at two-thirds of the height of the posts. The loose tops of some of the rods are then crossed and tied together to form rib vaults, which function as 'the skeleton of a thatched roof'; others between the posts are crossed and tied together to produce 'the exact form of the Gothic arch'. Rods 'thrust into the ground below, and bound to the arch above' would either be 'filled with twigs wattled through them' to create a kind of 'basket-work' wall, or left partly bare to let in light, thus anticipating 'the slender bars of stone, called Mullions, which constitute the framework of glass, in all Gothic windows'. The door would stand recessed between the smaller of two nested pointed arches, while the steeple or spire would be composed of 'eight long

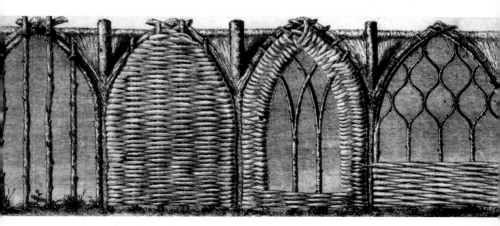

Basketwork wall, in Hall, 'On the Origin and Principles of Gothic Architecture', detail of plate IV.

and straight poles thrust into the ground' and angled to produce 'a very acute octagonal pyramid'. Hall surmises that originally steeples rested near, rather than atop, rustic churches, serving either as 'mere ornament' or 'to support a bell'. Later 'an architect would naturally think of raising it in the air, by placing it on the summit of a tower' to be widely visible.[26]

Having thus unearthed the roots of the basic forms of Gothic architecture, Hall turns to its ornaments, proposing that there are but two kinds, both of which 'may be traced to the effects of time upon the materials employed in the construction of our rustic fabric; one set being connected with the vegetation of the rods, and the other with their death and consequent decay'. Willow's tendency to take root and sprout would have resulted in a partly living rustic edifice whose buds and foliage became the models for the crockets and finials of stone Gothic architecture. The death of some of the willow rods, on the other hand, would result in peeling bark. Curling up before falling off, such bark gave rise to what Hall calls the 'cusp' ornamentation of

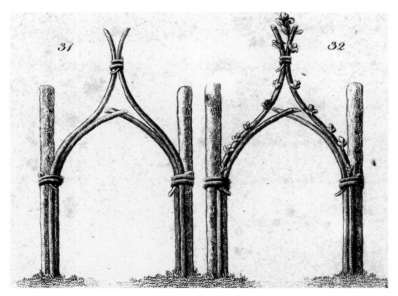

Living crockets, in Hall, 'On the Origin and Principles of Gothic Architecture', detail of plate V.

 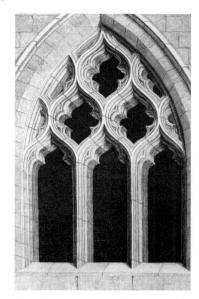

Cusp ornaments of peeling bark on willow rod mullions, in Hall, 'On the Origin and Principles of Gothic Architecture', detail of plate VI.

some Gothic windows – two curved lines meeting at a point, which are often combined into trefoils and other complex forms. An 'architect of genius', he is certain, observed this phenomenon and imitated it in stone.[27]

In spring 1792, desiring to put his theory to the test, Hall began, with the help of a cooper from Berwickshire named John White, to build a model willow church on his property. Its elements were based on existing works of stone Gothic architecture, and it was completed in the winter of 1793. Many of the willow rods, Hall tells us, took root and produced 'tufts of leaves' on the door arches. In the autumn of 1796 he observed 'one entire cusp formed by the bark in a state of decay, in a place corresponding exactly to those we see executed in Gothic works'.[28] The Scottish artist Alexander Carse painted Hall's fantastical edifice in 1792 or 1793. In this lovely watercolour (see overleaf) we see willow bent, tied and woven to create pointed arches, window mullions and tracery, and simple walls. Through the open doorway of the nave we glimpse clustered willow rods branching to support

Alexander Carse, *Willow Cathedral*, c. 1792, watercolour and gouache.

the thatched roof, and, outside, a leafing spire. The naturalness and simplicity of this rustic vegetable edifice are suggested by the backdrop of trees and foreground vegetation, while its method of construction is demonstrated by the simply clad figure, either Hall or White, who appears to be binding a cluster of willow wands together. An elaborate finial resting on a wooden post before him will, we imagine, eventually adorn the unfinished root of the transept.

In 1813 Hall published a long book on his theory, *Essay on the Origin, History, and Principles, of Gothic Architecture*, lavishly illustrated with 90 engravings. The frontispiece, while based on Carse's watercolour, illustrates the completed structure of his backyard willow cathedral. The book expands the argument of the 1797 essay in several ways, most significantly through accounts and illustrations of the willow origins of a great variety of Gothic structures and ornaments. Hall also cites a number of medieval manuscripts which suggest that the first Christian churches erected in England were built of '*rods*'; he concludes that 'the first apostles of Christianity in this island did actually perform divine service in oratories made of wicker-work', a mode of construction he deems 'most natural for men to have recourse to, in a wooded state of the country, who were devoid of the tools and of the skill required to construct more substantial fabrics'. Reverence for tradition, he supposes, inspired later builders to take 'the primitive *church of wattles*' as 'the prototype of a cathedral'.[29]

Hall was the first – and will probably remain the only – scholar to insist on the willowy origins of Gothic architecture. His conviction was regarded by some of his contemporaries, including Friedrich von Schlegel, as 'vulgar functionalism' and 'botanical utilitarianism'.[30] Hall's analysis, though, was as much poetic as rooted in practice. In his first publication on the willow cathedral he argued that works of art which imitate nature so closely as to include even its imperfections 'influence the mind of the spectator' as powerfully 'when founded on fiction as on reality. For we judge of such a work, as we do of a romance, in which we are scarcely less interested than if we believed it to be true.'[31] The willow cathedral is indeed a romantic fantasy, a living architecture weaving together pagan past and Christian present, and a community of people out of a collection of willow wands.

In recent years collectives like Sanfte Strukturen (Soft Structures) have also tried to create community through living willow edifices, including a 'Weidendom' (willow cathedral) in Rostock, Germany. In a less ecclesiastical but equally fantastic vein, the contemporary American artist Patrick Dougherty has produced a number of large-scale willow sculptures that have been compared to beehives, castles, cocoons, garden follies, haystacks, nests, teapots and towers. These collaborative site-specific works, each produced with a team of helpers over three weeks, lie somewhere between basketry and architecture. Like Hall's wattle church, they weave people as well as willow together through the making of evocative, social 'woodland architecture'.[32] The living community they create, however, is ephemeral, and there is

Patrick Dougherty, *Summer Palace*, 2009, mostly willow with some sugar maple, beech, alder and green ash. Morris Arboretum, University of Pennsylvania.

something elegiac about these beautiful but empty edifices. Their air of abandonment contributes to viewers' sense of stumbling upon them by chance, like an empty bird's nest, evoking a pleasurable melancholy.

Summer Palace, constructed in 2009, is a bulbous, spiralling structure suggestive of turbans, onion domes, pastries and, above all, the spire of a whelk shell, as though its base was buried in the ground. Dougherty uses the glimpses of his works' interiors as 'a beckoning tool',[33] inciting actual and imaginary exploration. Entering through the top of the mouth into a mysterious natural architecture built to human scale but not inhabited by humans, only visited, we are literally drawn closer to nature, to imagining how other species dwell. This sense of dwelling is temporal as well as spatial: Dougherty's structures evoke not only other times (the imaginary *once was* of their inhabitation) but also other understandings of time, as cyclical rather than linear. These empty nests might be used again.

Toad Hall, constructed in 2005, immediately conjures up a host of pastoral childhood images, marshalled not only by the name, that of Toad's home in *The Wind in the Willows*, but also by the shape, which evokes boots (and the nursery rhyme *The Old Woman Who Lived in a Shoe*), hot-cross buns, haystacks, silos and even, some say, rabbits. The earthen floor and stick structure suggest warrens as well as nests, and the willow tunnel through which one enters, a kind of secret passage, leads to the discovery of a lost world. The spectre of lost worlds is also raised by the work's architectural references. Deliberately mimicking the Spanish missions built in California in condensed form, here with a miniature campanile and nave,[34] *Toad Hall* does not separate the history of colonialism and religious imperialism from nature, but considers human culture's effect upon the landscape.

Moving from the outside world to the interior, we find that if willow has been used to create evocative architectures, it has also, since Greco-Roman antiquity at least, been used to furnish them. Pliny the Elder, for example, considered white (peeled) willow 'extremely

opposite: Patrick Dougherty, *Toad Hall*, 2005, willow saplings, 8.2 m high. Santa Barbara Botanic Garden.

Roman lady at her toilette, relief, second century CE.

suitable for luxurious easy chairs'.[35] These woven willow chairs usually had high, curved backs and seat cushions, and were associated with the sedentary lifestyle of women, scholars and philosophers (military and government officials, in contrast, used less comfortable curule seats while working).[36] A second-century relief shows a woman at her toilette in a willow *cathedra*, in which a variety of weaving techniques have been used to create a decorative pattern.

In the early twentieth century, the aptly named Gustav Stickley popularized woven willow furniture in America and was the founder of the 'Craftsman' style in architecture and furniture. Influenced by the British Arts and Crafts movement, he advocated truth to materials and simplicity of design. Today he is best known for his heavy wood furniture, but starting in 1903 he introduced lighter wicker pieces into his repertoire. Stickley disdained 'the usual opaque enamel' with which willow was often treated in wicker furniture, preferring the natural finish.[37] He was drawn to willow not just for its colouring, lightness and formal flexibility, however; its use in Native American cultures gave it an air of authenticity he valued while its role in contemporary agriculture and design made it modern. The *Craftsman Magazine* ran articles on Native American willow architecture, willow baskets, the willow-growing industry in America and contemporary European willow design (as well as their own, of course). One article described woven willow chairs as possessing 'the same qualities of intimacy and charm as a basket',[38] though two rather grand Stickley willow armchairs from *c.* 1910 are more imposing than such quotidian containers. Evoking thrones and even architecture with their window-like openings and the balconied arms of the chair on the left, they would originally have been upholstered with velvet or velour cushions. Despite their regal air, Stickley believed the willow itself would suggest nature more forcefully than culture: he described the variable golden honey-brown or greenish colours of the chairs as retaining 'all the sparkle seen in the thin branches of the growing tree as it becomes lustrous with the first stirring of the sap', and even more lyrically as having 'all the intangible silvery shimmer of water in moonlight'.[39]

William Morris, one of the founders of the English Arts and Crafts movement and an advocate for a return to pre-industrial manufacturing techniques and non-alienated labour, was drawn to the willow as both a symbol and a material. It is not surprising that Morris should

Gustav Stickley, willow armchairs, models #87 and 17D, *c.* 1910.

have loved the poetic and practical willow; in many ways it framed his life and career in literature, design and politics. His supposed first poem, read to his friends at Oxford in 1854, was called 'The Willow and the Red Cliff', and when he died his body was placed on a bed of moss in a funeral cart decorated with willow branches, which was drawn for three miles through hedgerows to Kelmscott church.[40] In the 1870s and '80s he created a number of willow-patterned fabrics and wallpapers that can be read as emblems of his artistic and socialist project.

In 1873 Morris designed *Tulip and Willow*, a furnishing fabric. When he first printed it using aniline (chemical) dyes, he found the result too garish and began studying indigo discharge dyeing, using chewed willow twigs to apply the indigo.[41] Having slowly perfected the use of older vegetable dye techniques and block printing on textiles, Morris moved his manufacturing to Merton Abbey Works on the river Wandle in 1881, a site described by his daughter May as deeply willowy: 'always the long willow-leaves pressed against the shabby windows . . . The whole impression of the place was sparkling water with sweet flowered margin, poplars and willows.'[42] There, in 1883, Morris returned to *Tulip and Willow* and, ten years after his first attempt, produced a cotton fabric across which blue-green willow spirals lace around extravagant white and yellow tulips.

The art historian Caroline Arscott has argued that *Tulip and Willow* alludes to the nineteenth-century architect and art critic Gottfried Semper's well-known theory of ornament. Historically, according to Semper, patterns have derived from craft techniques; structural elements in one medium were carried over into another as ornament. In *Tulip and Willow*, the blue stems of the recognizable willow branches, which are bent in regular curves and systematically woven over and under the yellow tulip stems and the willow leaves, suggest the form and process of basket as well as textile manufacture. Morris's fabric pattern, then, in its allusion to weaving, willow-applied indigo and the willowy site of its production, reintroduces something of the 'physical substantiality' of the useful object and its mode of

Morris and Co.,
Tulip and Willow,
fabric, designed 1873,
printed 1883, block-
printed and indigo
discharge on cotton.

fabrication into the Victorian commodity. No longer divorced from its scene of manufacture, the fabric functions, at least imaginarily, to overcome the alienation of modernity.[43]

In 1874, the year after his first attempt to print *Tulip and Willow,* Morris produced a wallpaper called *Willow* (see overleaf), in which leaves frond across a pale ground. The stems obey a rather strict geometry: at regular intervals intersecting serpentine lines rise up in columns, offshoots of which form symmetrical curves on either side. Against the flat, undifferentiated grey-brown ground in this example (all Morris wallpapers were available in various colour schemes), the interpenetrating willow foliage creates a shallow space. Morris's daughter described this paper, which hung in her father's bedroom at Kelmscott Manor in a blue print, as 'restful and pleasant'. It captures a sense of shadiness without shadows, cool repose without stasis.[44]

In 1887 Morris returned to willow in wallpaper, creating the *Willow Bough* pattern, which would eventually decorate the bedroom of

Morris and Co.,
Willow wallpaper,
1874, print on
paper

Morris and Co.,
Willow Bough
wallpaper, 1887,
block-printed
in distemper colours
on paper.

Jane Morris, his wife, at Kelmscott. May recalled her father describing willow leaf forms to her while designing the pattern, showing her leaves on the grounds and in Gerard's *Herbal*.[45] The geometry of the stems is somewhat loosened here, and complicated by different colours: against a creamy ground, warm brown stems from which pale grey-green leaves shoot snake upwards from the bottom right to the top left, while green-brown stems and leaves run from the bottom left to the top right, creating a diagonal lattice. Unlike *Willow* or *Tulip and Willow*, *Willow Bough* seems infused with light and space. The woven willow pattern creates an airy bower, for the scale of Morris's willow designs has shifted from that of the object (the basket) to that of the garden through the infinitely extendable trellis.

A few years later, Charles Rennie and Margaret Macdonald Mackintosh spatialized Morris's two-dimensional conjuring of a willow bower when they designed the Willow Tea Rooms, which opened in October 1904 in Glasgow's Sauchiehall Street. Catherine Cranston, the proprietor, was an advocate of the temperance movement and opened several tearooms in Glasgow for women and men seeking an alternative to the public house. Sauchiehall literally means 'house

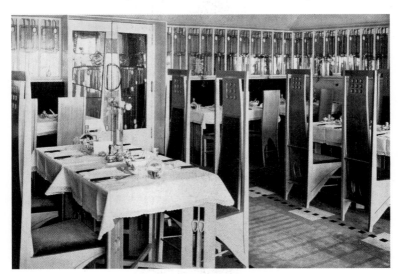

Room de Luxe, Willow Tea Rooms, Glasgow.

Room de Luxe,
Willow Tea Rooms.

of willows',[46] and the Mackintoshes imagined the establishment as a willow grove where atmosphere rather than alcoholic beverages would intoxicate patrons. Willows are not directly represented anywhere, but rather evoked through the stylized surroundings. Each chamber had its own decorative scheme in which the theme of willow was expressed through the repeated shape of the willow leaf, the 'high, spindly backs' of the chairs which resembled 'a forest of young willow trees',[47] airy colours and light-dappling mirrors and glass.

The heart of the Willow Tea Rooms was the Room de Luxe, a white, grey, silver, pink and purple bower for ladies only. A frieze of vertical mirrors running below the ceiling, inlaid with coloured glass and leaf-shaped leading, cast myriad reflections of the slender verticals reiterated throughout the room in the white wooden fillets between the

opposite: Margaret Macdonald Mackintosh, *O Ye, All Ye That Walk in Willowwood*, 1902, oil on gesso on board with twine, glass and enamelled glass beads.

mirrors, the cut-outs in the table legs and the tall, silvery chair backs. This 'jewel-like', sensuous, all-female realm was a kind of 'gossamer boudoir', inviting private reverie in a semi-public space.[48] The focal point of the room was a gesso panel by Margaret Macdonald Mackintosh, *O Ye, All Ye That Walk in Willowwood*, the title of which is a quotation from a poem by Dante Gabriel Rossetti about the remembrance of lost love, whose shades walk amongst willow trees. Mackintosh's panel depicts three elongated, white-faced women in flowing robes on a pale background. The elegant lines of their raiment, studded with coloured glass beads, are difficult to distinguish from those suggesting the pendent tresses of the willows, and the confusion between women and willow is exacerbated by the green ellipse, like a leafy lens, framing the central dryad. One enraptured reviewer described the panel's 'star-like', 'mysterious light' as weaving a veil around 'the faces and forms of the women walking silently, as if enthralled, through the willow grove'.[49] Rather than hanging on the wall, it sat at floor level in a large, white frame suggesting a doorway as much as a picture frame, thus placing the diaphanous, serene vision of willowwood within reach of the tea drinkers.

Haunting reveries can be evoked by everyday objects as well as works of art. In the Willow Tea Rooms patrons were served, unsurprisingly, on willow pattern china,[50] the same design that filled Aesthetic houses likely to be decorated with William Morris wallpapers, and the subject of the next chapter.

three

Pattern of Romance and Mystery

ꩠ

N o book treating the cultural history of the willow could
ignore the willow pattern in china. After it first appeared
in the 1790s it quickly became, and has remained, the world's
most popular dish decoration. Over the last 200 years, it has been
produced by over 350 potteries in England alone, as well as others
in Australia, Belgium, China, Denmark, France, Finland, Germany,
the Netherlands, Ireland, Japan, Mexico, Norway, Poland, Scotland,
Sweden, the United States and Wales.[1] It has been globally distributed – carried by colonizers into other lands if not exported there
directly – and used, reused and copied everywhere, from Staffordshire
to New Zealand, from the White House to the Solomon Islands. Only
recently has its star begun to wane: although still produced, it is no
longer a household staple; its domain has become largely that of
impassioned collectors.

The standard, or 'classic', willow pattern is usually blue and white,
and depicts a Chinese waterside scene framed within one or two
ornamental borders (see overleaf). On the right side of the design a
'mansion' with upturned roofs, and sometimes one or more smaller
structures, sits amidst a lush garden filled with diverse types of tree.
Among these one bearing large, spherical fruit is particularly prominent.
A few rocks and hillocks are visible in the garden, but the ground in
front of the main edifice is quite flat. A white path leading up to the
mansion breaks near the bottom of the scene and is crossed by a
zigzag fence which disappears at the edge of a river or lake. Just above

Wedgwood willow pattern plate, *c.* 1920, transfer-printed earthenware.

the fence grows a gnarled willow tree, whose pendent branches are loaded with springtime catkins. Its trunk is covered with fungus-like growths and leans heavily to the left, over a bridge that leads to a small island. Little figures carrying different objects cross to the island, above which a boat can be seen on the tranquil waters. One or more islands above the boat may be dotted with trees, rocks, hills and small buildings. At the top, two birds seem to fly towards each other.

There are countless minor variations in the standard willow patterns of different potteries – in the shape and size of the birds, the type of boat and whether or not there is a figure on it, the number of arches on the bridge, the number of branches on the willow, the arrangement of the garden and so on – but the basic layout is always more or less

Spode willow pattern plate, *c.* 1820s, transfer-printed.

the same. What is it about this seemingly innocuous scene – a quaint Chinese landscape – that captured the world's imagination and gave rise not only to centuries of dining-table dominion but also countless works of literature and art that tell its story, explore its forms and investigate its cultural legacy?

First produced by the English pottery Spode in the 1790s, the willow pattern is a curious artefact born of cross-cultural encounter. The design draws on motifs found in hand-painted Chinese export porcelain but combines them into a novel and enigmatic arrangement transfer-printed onto earthenware made to imitate porcelain. As a mass-produced and mass-marketed commodity with a mechanically printed design, willow pattern china can be seen as an emblem of industrialization and globalization. It must be considered such, however, in light of the precedent set by the history of porcelain manufacture in China – the industry with which 'willow' was designed to compete.

While the Chinese have manufactured and exported porcelains for over a thousand years – first to the Middle East and later to Europe and beyond – what interests us is the white porcelain with cobalt blue underglaze painting first produced in the fourteenth century: the famous blue and white wares that became the most widely distributed, mass-produced commercial objects prior to the Industrial Revolution and have been called the first 'global artifacts'.[2] In efficiency of manufacturing, scale of production and global reach, the kilns at Jingdezhen in Jiangxi province – the 'porcelain capital' of China – were industrialized to modern European standards long before the Industrial Revolution.

By the sixteenth century, Jingdezhen's official and private kilns employed 10,000 workers, and by the eighteenth yearly exports to Europe, never mind domestic and other export trade, are estimated to have been around a million pieces (several hundred thousand of which went to Britain), furnished by the more than 3,000 imperial and private kilns operating.[3] The global scale of Jingdezhen's enterprise required the sort of factory organization and division of labour associated with the Industrial Revolution. Different departments were devoted to specific ceramic forms (such as teacups) or processes (sketching designs, painting, glazing and so on), and even the painting was parcelled out. As one English traveller reported,

> One man traces the outline of a flower, another of a pagoda, while a third is at work upon a river or a mountain; a fourth receives it to draw the circle around the edge, while a fifth puts on the pigments according to these marks.[4]

With each worker's task so specific, a single item might have been subject to as many as 72 processes in its manufacture.[5]

Most hand-painted Chinese blue and white export porcelain was decorated with landscape scenery, which frequently included hills, streams, pavilions, bridges, boats, birds and/or plants. Because of the high demand for 'sets' of china, most exports to the West were, by the early nineteenth century, limited to a few patterns, a number of which inspired the willow pattern. Many designs featured a willow tree, and by the late eighteenth century 'willow' had become a generic term in Britain signifying Chinese landscape designs.[6] An octagonal plate is typical of the porcelain exported to the West (see overleaf). In this case, an elaborate double border frames a riverside scene. In the foreground two figures cross a bridge, to the left of which is the near-obligatory weeping willow whose branches seem to waft in a gentle breeze. In the middle ground a tongue of rock curling towards the water is framed by a slightly wonky pavilion on the right, a low building on stilts to the left and two trees above. At the top left, a small hut rests on an outcrop of land or an island. The plate exhibits a variety of painting techniques and hands, and is typical of export porcelain in what some Westerners considered its 'odd mixture or jumbling together of so many separate and heterogeneous objects',[7] but it is also unified by a lack of shadows and the monochrome palette.

Despite its resemblance to several common export porcelain patterns, however, the willow pattern is a peculiarly English invention. In the late eighteenth century, Staffordshire potteries developed new types of ceramics and a printing process that allowed them to offer relatively cheap imitations of hand-painted blue and white Chinese porcelain. Josiah Wedgwood's 'Pearl White' ware, invented in the 1770s, first offered an alternative to the yellowish 'creamware' that Staffordshire potteries had been producing since the 1750s. In the 1790s Spode began manufacturing bone china, also white, which provided another suitable surface to compete with Chinese exports. As importantly, Spode perfected transfer printing in the 1780s, which entails taking a print made from a copperplate engraving onto tissue paper and transferring the inked design to a ceramic surface. Using cobalt imported from Northern Europe, the Staffordshire potteries were able to produce their own blue and white wares.

Some British firms, such as Caughley, first made hand-painted imitations of Chinese porcelains to compete with imports. Caughley then became the first pottery to manufacture blue printed patterns, but offered them on porcelain, not earthenware.[8] Thomas Minton, an apprentice engraver at Caughley, engraved several popular Chinese patterns for the firm, including a recognizable precursor to the willow pattern, which features most of the elements of classic willow but omits the fence, path, bridge and figures. The Caughley engraving on the right, from the 1770s or 1780s, reverses the pattern as found on the export porcelain, on the left; it also renders the space more navigable to the Western eye by reducing the scale of the boat and birds,

Octagonal plate, early 19th century, Chinese export porcelain.

Left: Detail of 'Two Birds' pattern plate, *c.* 1780s, Chinese export porcelain; *Right*: engraved copper printing plate from Caughley Porcelain Factory, *c.* 1780s.

solidifying the cloud-like rocks at the upper left of the Chinese painting, regularizing the architecture, articulating the foreground landscape, and making the whole design slightly more airy.[9]

Like their Jingdezhen counterparts, Staffordshire potteries operated on a kind of assembly-line system. Transfer printing was a complicated affair. A multi-step process, it began with heating the engraved plate and moistening the tissue paper with water and soap, the greasiness of which allowed the ink to transfer to the ceramic surface. After the tissue paper and plate were run through a roller press by a printer, the paper was removed from the plate and passed to a 'cutter', who snipped the various elements of the pattern apart. A 'transferer' next carefully arranged the pieces of tissue on whatever piece of pottery was to be decorated, then rubbed the back of the paper, first with a piece of felt to secure its position, and next, more forcefully, with a brush to transfer the ink from the paper to the porous earthenware or bone china. The paper was then washed off and the piece fired in the kiln, after which it was glazed and re-fired. In the finished piece the pattern showed through, and was protected by, the glaze. A pearlware platter from an unidentified Staffordshire pottery gives us a glimpse of this cut-and-paste process: used both for trial printing and as a copybook, the dish is covered with transfer prints of pieces of the willow pattern, borders as well as motifs, each labelled with its particular form (saucer, plate, cup and so on).

Transfer printing does not produce the crispness of prints on paper, as the ink and glaze melt and blur during firing to create a soft, delicate texture 'floating in a glassy film', giving it an immediacy akin to painting.[10] Despite these sensual and somewhat unpredictable effects, some considered the willow pattern's mechanical reproduction a 'mindless' copying and the cause of its aesthetic failure, one particularly visible in the willow itself. Although a 'copy-book or catalogue' approach to composition was well established in eighteenth- and nineteenth-century Chinese art, painting manuals stressed that in rendering willows 'it is important to take into account how the wind stirs and spreads the willow leaves'.[11] To Western connoisseurs, the willow pattern seemed stilted and vulgar in comparison to hand-painted Chinese porcelains. One mid-nineteenth-century commentator described the pattern as an 'unfeeling copy of a Chinese pagoda, bridge, and willow-tree "in blue print"'.[12] The curator Crosby Forbes expressed his dismay that while a Chinese painter would let us '"see"

Dish, c. 1870, willow pattern transfer-prints on pearlware.

the breeze gently blowing' the branches of the willow, the willow pattern offers us instead a 'stationary, fixed object'; similarly, the birds seemed to him like 'paper cut-outs pasted onto the sky', which, technically, they were.[13]

Others judged the pattern's problem a failure of perspective: the American ethnologist William Churchill considered it 'almost unde-cipherable because it lacks the particular quality of perspective which we have learned to expect' and which represented, he argued, 'the whole difference between Orient and Occident'.[14] The aerial viewpoint the plate implies was not unfamiliar to Western viewers, but some critics, including Charles Dickens, regarded it as neither 'wholesome' nor 'natural', unlike 'faultless perspective'.[15] Without entering into details, the twentieth-century ceramics historian Warren Cox was absolute in his dismissal: 'Nothing could better exemplify the utter dearth of aesthetic consciousness than the stupid copying of this design which lacks every element of true Chinese painting and any real claim to beauty whatsoever.'[16]

Even the willow pattern's defenders have long acknowledged 'its want of artistic beauty'.[17] Its appeal may lie, rather, in its oddities, which have been noted, and mocked, by many. The disproportion-ately large spherical fruits – which have been variously identified as oranges, apples, persimmons, pomegranates and peaches – were classified by nineteenth-century satirists as the products of a 'pump-kin tree' or the 'PUDDING-TREE of Linnaeus'.[18] Odd hybrids abound: the robes of the figures on the bridge are shaped like fishtails, sug-gesting a procession of mermaids or mermen, while the willow sports, in Dickens's words, 'foliage of blue ostrich features'.[19] Other features create 'an enticing sense of menace'. In addition to discrepancies of scale and perspectival disjunctions, the classic pattern is 'replete with psychological conflicts, problems of access, lurking dangers'. The path is blocked and broken by the zigzag fence; the mansion's staircase is blocked by the central column; the willow inhibits access to the bridge and the 'grotesquely laden' fruit tree towering above the mansion 'poses an obvious and immediate threat to the safety of the building'. The two borders together may even create a ring of snarling guardian beasts or *taotie*, with round eyes flanking a snarling muzzle. Willow expert David Quintner suggests that perhaps the West's 'undying fascination' with the pattern is due to its 'subliminal and unresolved problems, its inexplicability'.[20]

Some of the strange features of the pattern might be read as responses to contemporary events and phenomena, including the introduction of exotic fruits like oranges to Britain, the popularization of aerial views along with the practice of ballooning, and the mania for *chinoiserie*. However, just over forty years after the willow pattern was first produced – long enough for many generations to have lived with it – accounts purporting to identify the narrative it supposedly depicts as an old Chinese tale began to circulate, presumably in response to both its popularity and its mysteriousness. In 1838 Mark Lemon published a 'true history' of the 'hieroglyph' it formed. This satirical account is prefaced by a history lesson: under the reign of the Emperor Fo, Lemon tells us, the philosopher Fum introduced the doctrine of the transmigration of souls. Against this backdrop unfolds the romance of Si-so, daughter of the wealthy merchant Chou-chu, and the minstrel Ting-a-ting, who serenades her from a boat on the Slo-Flo. One night Chou-chu catches Si-so and Ting-a-ting trysting and decides to marry his daughter to a wealthy suitor. Ting-a-ting disguises himself as a pipe merchant and manages to convert Si-so to the doctrine of transmigration. On the day of the wedding, he impales Si-so upon his pigtail and plunges a dagger into his own heart. After the guests recover, they see two doves perched on the windowsill – the 'faithful pair' transformed into 'emblems of love and gentleness'. Chou-chu, the bridegroom and the bridegroom's father flee the scene and appear on the plate running across the bridge.[21] The racist 'humour' of Lemon's account is largely absent from what became the legend associated with the pattern, first published twelve years later.

In 1850 'The Story of the Common Willow-Pattern Plate' appeared. When too many people start to complain about a powerful and corrupt

Detail of *taotie*, Wedgwood willow pattern plate, *c.* 1920.

mandarin, he retires to the house pictured on the right-hand side of the plate, along with his daughter, Koong-see, and his secretary, Chang. A romance develops between the penniless Chang and the beautiful Koong-see in the estate's luscious gardens. The mandarin inevitably discovers their courtship; outraged, he builds the zigzag fence to keep Chang out. He also betroths his daughter to a much older, wealthy Ta-jin or duke, telling her that they will marry when the peach tree blossoms. The willow tree is currently in bloom, and functions in the tale as a vegetable clock counting down to the dreadful moment of unwanted, arranged marriage. Confined to her quarters, which overlook the water, Koong-see is surprised one night to find a message sent to her in a tiny boat. In it Chang threatens to drown himself when the willow blossom droops and the peach tree blooms. Koong-see responds with some practical advice: 'wise husbandmen gather the fruits they fear will be stolen'. She receives no further message and frets, particularly when her father presents her with a gift from the Ta-jin, a box of jewels.

On the day of the wedding, the mandarin and the duke, a military man, start the ceremonies with drinking. While they are tipsy, a stranger seeking alms – Chang in disguise – arrives and makes his way to Koong-see's rooms, from whence the pair flees with the box of jewels. The mandarin espies their flight and pursues them, which is pictured on the plate in the three figures on the bridge, the first Koong-see 'carrying a distaff, the emblem of virginity', followed by

Chang and the box of jewels, and lastly the mandarin, 'whose paternal authority and rage are supposed to be indicated by the whip which he bears in his hand'. The lovers are sheltered by Koong-see's former maid and her husband, the estate's gardener, in their 'humble tenement' across the bridge, where the marriage is performed and witnessed. Soldiers sent to search for the lovers by the Ta-jin are foiled by the maid, and Chang manages to steal a boat. The young couple sail along the Yangtze and find an island on which to settle, pictured at the top left of the plate. Discreetly selling the jewels in nearby towns, they build a house and grow crops. Chang then writes an acclaimed book on agriculture, and his renown leads the vengeful Ta-jin to him. Soldiers attack the island and Chang is stabbed to death; Koong-see, unable to live without her lover, sets the house on fire and perishes in the flames. The gods then curse the cruel duke 'with a foul disease' and, taking pity on the lovers, transform them into 'two immortal doves, emblems of the constancy which had rendered them beautiful in life, and in death undivided'.[22]

The legend is in many ways horrific: a tale of incarceration, theft and brutal murder as much as young love. Written in the aftermath of the first Opium War, it reflects British concerns with the Chinese power structure. The literary scholar Patricia O'Hara has argued that the 'conventional conflicts of Western romance (youth vs. age, romantic love vs. filial duty)' are politically charged in the willow pattern story, which 'expresses the assumption that what Europe understands to be Chinese culture should yield to the powers (youth, love, literature) of the romance' and, allegorically, to 'the British intrusion into the Celestial Empire'.[23] If the story is freighted with colonial significance, the material history of the pattern is equally so, with its global distribution through British travel and colonial expansion.

In his novel *Loss and Gain: The Story of a Convert* (1848), Cardinal Newman, who climbed Vesuvius in 1847, has a character remark, 'you find English crockery everywhere on the Continent. I myself found half a willow-pattern saucer in the crater of Vesuvius.'[24] A dala in the British museum offers a more ambiguous sign of British dominion.

Dalas, forehead ornaments worn by Solomon Islanders, traditionally consist of a disc cut from a large clamshell overlaid with a turtleshell fretwork; they are attached to the head by a plaited band. This example was acquired in 1900 by Charles Woodford, the first British resident commissioner of the Solomon Islands Protectorate, when he 'had to punish some natives for head hunting near Rubiana' and, taking them by surprise, was able to loot the village and acquire a number of artefacts including two dalas made from old plates.[25] Composed of a disc cut out of a faded willow pattern plate and covered with a revolving disc of turtleshell fretwork of exquisite delicacy, this hybrid object is the wonderfully creative result of a cross-cultural encounter. If the British imagined themselves as the young lovers vis-à-vis China's cruel patriarchs in the willow pattern legend, the story of this dala's acquisition casts the British commissioner in the role of the furious Ta-jin who, bent on his quest for treasure, destroys their island haven. In America, where President Martin Van Buren ordered willow for the White House in the 1830s, the pattern became a symbol of the young colony that defied its British parents, of anti-elitism in the rise of the secretary, and of female emancipation. Later it became associated with prohibition (the lovers are able to flee because Koong-see's father and the groom get drunk,[26] hence its appropriateness for the Willow Tea Rooms as well).

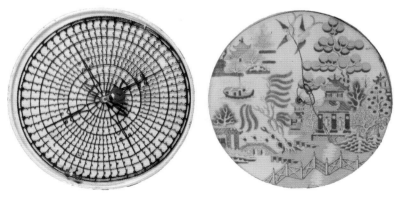

Dala ornament, 19th century, willow-pattern china plate overlaid with turtleshell fretwork.

If the willow pattern was linked with colonialism, it was nevertheless also relevant to potentially violent domestic scenes. Lemon described the mansion as a 'curious construction' with its 'bow-window' over the lake 'admirably situated for FISHING, BATHING, OR SUICIDE', and pointed out the estate's birch, 'whose usefulness' to the 'married man' needs 'no commendation'.[27] Dickens saw the boat's mast as 'burglariously sticking itself into the foundations of a blue villa',[28] while another satirist described the scene as one so 'uncommonly queer' that the viewer must be 'tipsy, or mad' to take it seriously.[29] Many authors who wrote about the willow pattern legend stressed its unsettling features.

At the same time, the pattern's association with childhood and an innocent world of possibility was equally strong. Henry Wadsworth Longfellow's poem 'Kéramos' (1877), which offers a brief overview of world pottery, celebrates 'The willow pattern, that we knew / In childhood, with its bridge of blue.'[30] The pattern's homeliness was unquestioned: as one author put it, willow is 'mingled with our earliest recollections; it is like the picture of an old friend and companion whose portrait we see everywhere, but of whose likeness we never grow weary'.[31] Even Dickens described a willow plate encountered in an inn as a 'companion' which, like him (biblically speaking) was created from 'lumps of clay' and eventually turned out from its 'nursery and seminary' into the world.[32] Intriguingly, all these writers associate the willow pattern with lived experience, and with the first questions a child asks: 'Who is there, since the earliest dawn of intelligent perception, who has not inquisitively contemplated the mysterious figures on the willow-pattern plate?'[33]

The pattern's famous love story became the basis for numerous theatrical works. *The Mandarin's Daughter*, first performed in 1851 at the Strand Theatre in London, emphasizes the foreignness and supposed inferiority of the characters, who are introduced by Chim-Pan-See and who speak in atrocious puns: the mandarin, called He-Sing in this production, laments, 'My daughter gone! this is a heavy blow; / By her *faux pas* she's made her pa a foe.'[34] (One review astonishingly proclaims the dialogue 'far beyond the usual mark in point of brilliancy'.[35]) A comic opera called *The Willow Pattern Plate*, written by Basil Hood and set to music by Cecil Cook, is filled with even worse puns and names; it ran for 110 performances at the Savoy in 1901 and then went on tour. A Vaudeville musical called *The Willow Pattern Plate* ran from 1897 to 1913, and in 1914 Thomas Alva Edison made a short silent film about the legend which was followed, in 1931, by a Disney animated film, *The China Plate*.

If the story remained popular and the pattern, despite its hybridity, a 'national touchstone' for the English,[36] the aesthetic worth of both came into question in the late Victorian period. F. C. Burnand's comedy *A Tale of Old China* (1874), which revolves around a dealer duped into believing a willow pattern teapot is a precious Chinese antique, focuses on the pattern's relative valuations.[37] By then, connoisseurs widely dismissed the willow pattern as inferior to antique, hand-painted Chinese porcelain. Oscar Wilde's famous desire to 'live up to' his blue and white china nevertheless cemented the place of the willow pattern as well as blue and white porcelain in the culture of Aestheticism; both adorned Aesthetic interiors (along with Morris's willow pattern fabrics and wallpapers), and those who lived according to Aesthetic principles were mocked in *Punch* caricatures featuring effeminate willowy devotees suffering from 'chinamania' or vowing to live up to their collections (see overleaf).

The Egoist by George Meredith, first published in 1879, provides both a political and a literary critical take on the willow pattern and collecting. The novel is a complicated love story featuring the wealthy and handsome Sir Willoughby Patterne, the egoist of the title; Vernon Whitford, his dependent cousin and a scholar; Laetitia Dale, a poor local girl in love with and thoughtlessly encouraged by Sir Willoughby; and Clara Middleton, a young beauty who is aggressively courted by Sir Willoughby after he has been spurned in love by the fashionable and inaptly named Constantia Durham. The action takes place at the Patterne estate, where Dr Middleton has brought his daughter for a visit before the wedding. Clara is immediately dubbed a 'dainty

George Du Maurier, 'The Six-Mark Tea-Pot', *Punch*, 30 October 1880.

rogue in porcelain' by one of the local gentry, a phrase which discomfits Willoughby as it suggests a liveliness and volatility incompatible with the beautiful object reflective of his own glories he hoped to purchase for a bride. He becomes 'haunted by the phrase', tortured by its suggestion of a 'ripple over her features' that betokens 'innocent roguery, wildwood roguery', the consequences of which might be flight and shattered fantasies. Clara quickly learns to despise her monstrously narcissistic fiancé and struggles to free herself from her engagement. Determined not to be jilted again, he refuses to release her. Like Koongsee in the willow pattern legend, Clara finds herself trapped into an unwanted marriage and imprisonment on the Patterne grounds ('hedges and palings everywhere!'), ensnared by Willoughby's 'design', and abandoned by her father who is seduced by Willoughby's wine cellar and dismisses Clara's complaints as 'tea-cup tempests'.[38]

Clara's efforts to escape are noticed and assisted by various characters, one of whom comments that her wedding gift 'should have been the Willow Pattern'. Sir Willoughby, driven mad by the suggestion, proposes to Laetitia Dale, whose eyes have been opened to his faults and who refuses him. Finally, Willoughby's duplicity (or rather, his pattern of behaviour) is revealed to all, and Clara is freed. Laetitia accepts the humiliated Willoughby on condition of his submitting to her better judgement, while Clara marries Vernon, whom she has encountered many times in the lush gardens of the estate and with whom she has been in love all along. The book ends with a report of the pair honeymooning at Lake Constance.[39]

The novel's plot, then, doubles that of the willow pattern legend, pairing a young heiress with a poor scholar and the heir of the Patterne estate with a poor, literarily inclined neighbour – both porcelains, as it were, ending paired with coarser pottery. (Willoughby compares Laetitia's heart to 'potter's clay', while Vernon, 'pottered' after Willoughby, is perhaps an embodiment of one of the new English ceramics, a 'new kind of thing, nondescript, produced in England of late'.)[40] The text is relentless in its pottery analogies: characters are 'classed' as ceramics of differing qualities; broken engagements are likened to shattered porcelain. Shedding light on Willoughby's despotic treatment of women, *The Egoist* offers a culturally self-reflective riff on the willow pattern story and the supposed English superiority to the Chinese for which it had come to stand. Meredith uses the legend, O'Hara contends, 'as a mirror in which Victorian society is meant to find its own reflection: the collective British "we" are unmasked as being just as barbaric', especially in terms of the treatment of women, 'as the oriental "them"'.[41]

Other novels have taken up the legend's violent crimes, suggesting that imaginary indulgence in the patriarchal sadism of the willow legend is a large part of the pattern's appeal. In Robert van Gulik's novel of 1965, *The Willow Pattern: A Chinese Detective Story*, a shattered willow pattern vase is the key to solving several connected mysteries involving murder, women bought and sold, and sexual torture.[42] In a similarly sensational vein, W. J. Burley, famous for his Wycliffe mysteries and the television series based on them, used the willow pattern story as a model – and the garden as a model site – for crime in his book *Death in Willow Pattern* (1969). In the novel, the Leigh family's estate is home to a willow pattern folly, complete with mandarin's house and pagoda with upturned roofs, a giant willow, ornamental fence, island and boats, built around 1800 by an eccentric ancestor. Young girls in the neighbourhood have gone missing and the investigation reveals that the garden conceals a subterranean complex including a torture chamber. The willow 'folly', we learn, is an index of and accessory to the Leighs' madness; in its hidden depths their ancestor tortured, raped and murdered young girls. For his descendants the pattern of his madness seems an inescapable one. The 'willow' of the story, then, is a hereditary and narrative matrix, the garden folly its literally superficial manifestation.[43]

Burley's novel is particularly intriguing not only for its exploration of the sex and murder (as well as theft and substance abuse) that figure prominently in the willow pattern's reception history, but also because it appears to have been based on a particular variant of the willow pattern produced by Burleigh – a homophone of the author's name. The manufacturers Burgess and Leigh, also known as Burleigh, have produced willowware since the nineteenth century. The Burleigh blue willow pattern exhibits a number of distinctive features that seem to have inspired elements of Burley's mystery. Rock formations that resemble heaps of rubble appear on an island, to the side of the ornamental balustrade, and near the pavilion, and evoke the mounds of rubble marking the torture chamber's entrance and ventilation shafts. The figure standing beside the fence suggests the story's garden-haunting deaf mute, while the long package carried by one of the figures on the bridge could be one of the body bags removed by Leigh's servant.

Willow pattern literature, whether emphasizing domestic, colonial and/or military violence (see, for example, William Hamilton

Burleigh Ware willow pattern plate, *c.* 1920s, transfer print on earthenware.

Canaway's *The Willow Pattern War* of 1976), tends to take the side of the young lovers. A notable exception, however, is the Pulitzer Prize-winning poet James Merrill's 'The Willowware Cup' (1972), one of the most beautiful and evocative texts dealing with the pattern and its legend, which offers a non-heteronormative reading of the object and the story. In the poem, the speaker, whose sailor lover has just departed, identifies not with the daughter but the father who, he imagines, must 'have given up earthly attachments' in his grief, which is now fading; he will soon ask 'only to blend into a crazing texture' as does tattoo 'ink in flesh' when a lover departs. If the willow pattern suggests personal dissolution, fading into insignificance after the heightened sensibility of love and loss, it nevertheless also functions, like sadness and like a tattoo, as a 'blue anchor' linking lover and beloved, for 'Around its inner horizon the old odd designs / Crowd as before, and seem to concentrate on you.'[44] The image of willowware recurs several times in Merrill's *oeuvre*, and in the poem of 1978 *Mirabell: Books of Number*, the willow tree itself comes to stand for lonely repression: 'MANY THE OLD AUNT WHO WEEPS / INSIDE THE WILLOW'.[45]

Highbrow or popular, the literature of the willow pattern relies on our intimate familiarity with it, even as authors expose largely unrecognized elements and meanings. So too does the work of many contemporary ceramics artists who have engaged with the willow pattern and its legacy. Their art calls into question not only our understanding of the willow pattern but also of ceramics as a medium and ornament as a category, the fantasies of domesticity that blue and white china in general seems to stand for, and the fraught relationship between the willow pattern's industrialized production and the pastoral landscape it depicts.

Robert Dawson is a renowned ceramics artist whose limited edition *After Willow* china, produced by Wedgwood and based on their classic willow, foregrounds and intensifies the cropping, pasting and sampling techniques that informed the original willow design and transfer-print production, which are updated and galvanized by

Robert Dawson, *In Perspective Willow 1*, 1996, print on bone china.

digital manipulation that allows perspectival play. Two of his artworks specifically take up the question of the willow pattern's 'perspective' so dear to nineteenth-century commentators. In *In Perspective Willow 1* he rotates the pattern to give us a recessive view, which hovers on the surface of the white plate and creates a tension between its flatness and the *trompe-l'oeil* effect. In so doing, Dawson's piece calls attention to the ceramic surface as both a utilitarian one, when laid on the table, and an aesthetic one, when displayed upright on a shelf or a wall. Its simultaneous vertical and horizontal orientations desta - bilize the viewer's assumed position of mastery over simple crockery and challenge any dismissal of ornament as superficial.[46] Literalizing the fantasy of fixing the willow pattern's perspectival inaccuracies by offering a plausible recession, Dawson's work destabilizes the

Robert Dawson, *Willow Pattern with Uncertainty*, 2003, print on bone china.

viewer not only through its ambiguous orientation but also through its fulfilment of the ambivalent desire for both the familiar pattern and a 'corrected' version of it.

In *Willow Pattern with Uncertainty*, Dawson focuses on the mystery that surrounds the pattern and its narrative by blurring the focus, which is sharp only at the lower right edge of the border. Our familiarity with the pattern renders it instantly recognizable despite its near-complete invisibility; our veiled view, however, suggests that its significance as well as its details have faded into time and memory. One critic reads the plate's 'blurred and milky' appearance as a suggestion that it has 'bled into itself as a result of too many washes'.[47] Taken literally or figuratively, the willow pattern's simultaneous ubiquity and obscurity is the subject of Dawson's piece, which shows how that which is closest to us might exist largely unperceived and unknown.

The habitually unseen or unacknowledged side of domestic life is also explored by Karen Ryan in her 'Second Hand' series. The artist takes old plates and, by selective removal of parts of the decoration, uncovers texts hidden in and previously camouflaged by the image. The words she has found in the willow pattern include *beauty*, *love*, *hurt*, *beat*, *violent* and *lies*. The letters surface out of shapes in the pattern, so in *Lies* the lower bar of the 'E' is fashioned from brick courses while the stems of both the 'I' and the 'E' are created by the mansion's columns. The stem of the 'L' follows the edge of a pavilion while the bar stretches across the horizontal lawn to the house, and the 'S' follows the curves of a tree and hillocks in the garden. Despite its erasures and prominent text, the platter is instantly recognizable as willow, suggesting the mendacity inherent in the pattern's association with the ideal of home. Yet by enabling us to read the willow itself as an 'F', Ryan's piece allows us to see what flies in

Karen Ryan, *'Second Hand' Lies*, 2009, altered earthenware.

123

Paul Scott, *Scott's Cumbrian Blue(s)*, *A Millennium Willow for Sellafield or Plutonium is Forever (Well 24 Millennia Anyway)*, 2000, in-glaze decal on Royal Worcester bone china with gold lustre.

the pattern: the lovers who escape, who will nevermore by fenced in by the architecture of insincerity.

The ceramic artist and theorist Paul Scott has treated the willow pattern several times in his *oeuvre*. Two plates in his Cumbrian Blue(s) series revise the pattern to highlight how we treat nature and the landscape with industrial ruthlessness while still harbouring pastoral fantasies in our domestic interiors. In *A Millennium Willow for Sellafield or Plutonium is Forever (Well 24 Millennia Anyway)* of 2000 the mandarin's mansion has been replaced by the Sellafield nuclear power station and fuel-reprocessing plant, the enormous fruit tree by billows of steam and the boat by an industrial barge. The damaged-looking willow and pigeons rather than doves refer to the contamination of the site, which suffered a leak in 1957 and various safety breaches in subsequent decades. In 1998 all the pigeons within 10 miles of the plant had to be culled; having roosted in the towers, they were carrying radiation into the surrounding area.[48] Eyes on the *taotie* have been replaced with radiation warning signs and the skulls and crossbones of poison warnings below. The scene's desolate air is reinforced by the fleeing figures on the bridge carrying Japanese, German and Swiss flags, representing Sellafield's biggest customers abandoning the failing plant. The industrialization and recycling of images that enabled the production of the original willow pattern have reached a toxic apogee here.

The Fence Series, no. 4 (Willow) of 2006 illustrates how the logic of industrial capitalism has affected our relation to all landscape, not just the sites of plants and factories. In this work the zigzag fence has been

Paul Scott, *Scott's Cumbrian Blue(s), The Fence Series, no. 4 (Willow)*, 2006, in-glaze decal collage on ALP Lidköping porcelain plate with gold.

straightened out and now bars access to the willow, which is marked as property rather than serving as an evocative symbol. The birds are shrunk to be perspectivally plausible and are thereby rendered visually and narratively insignificant. Furthermore, rather than offering us a floating viewpoint, the plate grounds and excludes us literally and figuratively from imaginative exploration. The result is a controlled, barren landscape, drawing elements found within the picturesque garden of the original willow pattern to a sterile conclusion.

Other artists have taken the willow pattern as a symbol of industrialization and globalization to comment on the impoverishment of human experience they associate with those processes, and sometimes the violence as well. They have also used the pattern to commemorate specific historical events. There are visual precedents for this; in the willow pattern cover of an issue of the *New Yorker* of 14 November 1942, the willow tree serves as the hiding spot for a sniper. The pattern here is a battle scene: the boat becomes a destroyer, the lovebirds jet fighters; the zigzag fence is covered with barbed wire and the garden is full of cannon. It is not the lovers but the Japanese who flee across the bridge, shot at by ground troops as well as the sniper. Designed by Charles Addams, creator of *The Addams Family*, and reflecting ongoing events in the Sino-Japanese war, the cover inverts the image of domestic tranquillity that blue willow china conjures (just as *The Addams Family* inverts the ideal American family).

The Australian ceramic artist Gerry Wedd describes the willow pattern as 'a perfect serene place into which you can plant bombs'.[49] While Wedd and other artists insert extraneous elements that subvert some aspect of the willow pattern's narrative or 'image', others have found the pattern itself, with its fractured form and latent violence, volatile enough. In the willow pattern legend, the willow tree functions as a kind of timer counting down to the world-shattering flight of the lovers (Chang must rescue Koong-see before the willow leaves drop). Two contemporary artists have created ceramic ordnance that literalizes the imminently explosive quality of the willow pattern.

Charles Addams,
Blue Willow, design
for a *New Yorker*
cover, 1942.

Conrad Atkinson's willow pattern landmine (see overleaf) is one
of many such devices created by the artist, who began making his
biscuitware bombs in 1996 to call attention to the global landmine
crisis. Most of his mines are modelled on the Italian Valmara 69 bound-
ing mine which, when triggered by pressure on the pronged fuse cap,
launches an explosive that detonates around waist height, scattering
steel fragments that kill and maim. Atkinson considers landmines as
much an emblem of globalization as McDonald's, and this particular piece likens the global distribution of the willow pattern to that
of the hundreds of millions of anti-personnel mines around the
world (over 100 million laid, the rest waiting in storehouses). It also
calls attention to the military uses of ceramics, which today range
from body armour to missile nosecones. Ceramic bombs, though, have
been manufactured since the thirteenth century and were mass-produced
by the Americans and the Japanese during the Second World War, the

127

latter even devoting their most prestigious porcelain kilns, such as Arita, to the effort.[50] Although nearly 160 countries have signed the Ottawa Treaty banning anti-personnel landmines, the major producers, including China, Russia and the USA, have not. The on-going production, international sale and laying of landmines – not to mention other military ceramics – gives the term 'export porcelain' an alarming new meaning.

Atkinson has exhibited his mines, many of which are decorated with well-known images from the history of art as well as china

Conrad Atkinson, *Landmine (Blue Willow)*, 1996, glaze transfer with hand painting on Biscuitware ceramic land mine.

patterns, under the title 'Mining Culture', which captures the semantic polyvalence of his work.[51] Not only do his objects plumb the depths of history in their sampling of recognizable cultural achievements, they also suggest the role of mining (of clay and cobalt, for example) in ceramics manufacture in addition to visualizing the mines of the military-industrial complex that are most often hidden underground or in warehouses. More significantly, they make it impossible to dissociate the mass-production technologies that have helped disseminate high culture from their capacity to undermine its achievements. Or rather, they make it impossible to separate our aesthetic, commercial and military 'values' – they are gilded and glazed, glittering with the allure of the international commodity.

In a similar vein, Charles Krafft's porcelain grenade decorated with the willow pattern birds queries the distinction between the high and the low, or the fine and applied arts. Krafft, who is notorious for his 'Disasterware' (blue and white pottery resembling Delftware and depicting twentieth-century disasters), his Hitler teapots and his Spone® china made of human bones (combining ashes and urn in one memorial object), is primarily interested in the commemorative function of ceramics. His willow grenade is a delicate, hand-painted piece of porcelain that stands on a carved and polished wooden vase stand. Its smooth, spherical body invites touch and appreciation of its elegantly simple form, and seems an appropriately refined receptacle for the image of the metamorphosed lovers, whose sublimated silhouettes fit curiously well the shape of the explosive. The willow pattern birds are, as Quintner puts it, 'the design's linchpin', both narratively and visually (the composition looks bare without them).[52] Here they hover just beneath the grenade's linchpin. Krafft has produced numerous ceramic hand grenades and firearms, all made from moulds of actual weapons. The willow pattern grenade is based on an American Second World War hand grenade, the Beano T-13, which was developed for soldiers used to throwing baseballs, and thus was made to be the same size and weight. The object appeals to the hand as well as the eye. Thrown, the grenade would literalize the lovers' flight; the birds

Charles Krafft, *Hand Grenade with Birds*, 2010, painted porcelain.

Red Weldon Sandlin, *Behind Quiet Veils of the Blue Willow*, 2001, earthenware, wood and paint.

would be freed from their porcelain cage in a shattering romantic climax. In an odd alignment of the decorative and detonative arts, then, Atkinson and Krafft have created objects that are truly to be handled with care.

To end this chapter on a less violent note, let us turn to a work by Red Weldon Sandlin, whose *oeuvre* investigates traditional ceramic forms and the myths, rituals and stories with which they are invested. In *Behind Quiet Veils of the Blue Willow*, a wooden book serves as the base of a sculpted and painted ceramic assemblage incorporating a ginger jar and a teapot. Ginger jars (in which the Chinese exported crystallized ginger) are round-bodied, lidded porcelain pots whose pleasingly full shapes have long appealed to Western still-life painters. In China the jars were used as containers for spices, oils and other foods in addition to ginger, and were symbolically coded according to colour. A ginger jar with a white ground was a traditional wedding gift, and in Sandlin's piece the blue and white jar and teapot function as the symbolic foundations of domestic harmony.

Like the willow pattern legend, Sandlin's piece revolves around the suspicious mandarin, whose eyes literally direct us around the work, and the blossoming romance between his daughter and his secretary, which is born and which flourishes literally behind his back – the heads of the lovers are painted opposite the Mandarin's face on the backside of the lower half of the jar. The romance unfurls around the pregnant form of the pot; key moments in the story – Koong-see sending messages to Chang, the lovers' flight across the bridge, their escape via boat – appear in indented relief 'windows' set into the jar, as if the lovers are literally imaged dipping into the ginger jar itself, which becomes a metaphor for the sticky sweets and spices hidden in its eroticized interior. Above the jar, the twig-handled teapot forms a perch on which the half-metamorphosed lovers may momentarily rest. It can be lifted up and carried away like the lovers by the gods, and invites the viewer/reader to ensure the lovers' escape.

Sandlin has repeatedly likened the teapot to the book – both are filled with leaves that can be read; in her words, a book 'contains stories, information, and lessons. A teapot, metaphorically, holds ideas that are filtered, brewed, steeped, and poured out for fulfilment and understanding.'[53] We will explore the literature of the willow, and the fulfilments and understanding it offers, in the next chapter.

four
Tree of Prose and Poetry
🦂

P oetry and prose from East and West reveal the vast rhetorical range of willow. Poets have used it to figure the spectrum of emotions and human subjectivity itself, and willow recurs as a remarkably flexible motif in prose, seemingly germane to every genre – mystery, horror, fantasy, romance, children's books and 'high' literature. Examination of the willow motif in key texts reveals the suppleness of this tree of tropes, which can signify joy, grief, evil, forgiveness, the passage of time, environmental consciousness and much more.

In the West, willow is intimately associated with poetry. The ancient Greeks called it both ἰτέα and *helíke*,[1] the latter linking willow with Helicon, the mountain abode of the nine Muses and its flowing waters. And the sound of the wind whistling through willow leaves – the wind in the willows – has long been considered synonymous with poetic inspiration. It is no coincidence that the linguist and literary theorist Roman Jakobson chose the motif of a girl passing under a willow, a trope from Slavic folklore, to explain the poetic function of language. In his example, the willow becomes an image of the girl; it does not lose its botanical reference, but poetically gains meaning, becoming a 'double-sensed message'. The creation of this ambiguity is key to language becoming art, splitting sound and sense and opening up semantic possibilities by creating links between unlike things or realms.[2] As we will see, willow connects numerous realms and is an especially apt figure for poetic imaging.

The French philosopher Gaston Bachelard invoked several examples of the willow as enabling passages between poetically charged sites in his study of poetic images: 'the child, playing endlessly under the willows, goes from one meadow to another, master of two worlds, braving the tumultuous water. How many images have their natural origin there!'[3] In German *Weide* means willow and field or meadow; in French the words *saule* (willow) and *sol* (soil, ground) are also close. Bachelard reveals that willow, frequently found at the edges of watercourses and linked to them by habit and name (*sal-lis*, close to water), serves as a threshold between earth and water. It is also a ladder between earth and sky, lifting the poet or the child up into the air: the adolescent Chateaubriand set up his 'seat, like a nest', in one of the willows on the family estate, and 'there, isolated between heaven and earth, [he] spent hours among the warblers' with an imaginary nymph, a muse beautiful as the fresh dew, the nightingale's song and the murmur of the breeze, immortalized in the poetic prose of his *Memoirs from Beyond the Grave*.[4]

A beautiful image in Princess Marthe Bibesco's *Isvor: Country of Willows*, a memoir about her impossible desire to belong fully to a Romania where, 'from a distance, every village looks like a clump of willows', captures the willow's elemental shapeshifting:

> the wind rose without one's noticing, and then, one saw it racing. The reeds of the pond bent over, and then the willows went off all at once in the same direction, their leaves turned up and showing silver, off like arrows, like little white fish! The fisherman's tree, where the nets are hung, has caught thousands of whitebait![5]

Bridging earth, water and sky, the limber figure of the willow serves, in many texts, as a trope for other thresholds – between nature and culture, childhood and adulthood, idyll and exile. We will begin our investigation of willowy literature in the East where, as in the European tradition, the willow is linked to poets, women and sorrow.

Detail of Zhao Lingrang (attr.), *Lake Retreat among Willows*, mid-13th century, ink and colour on silk.

In China, the willow has long been intimately linked with scholars and poets, who 'would amble along the rivers and lakes where this tree grows, seeking inspiration'. The Jin Dynasty poet Tao Yuanming or 'Master of the Five Willows' named himself after the trees that grew around his country home, and depictions of such willowy writers' retreats abound.[6] The painting *Lake Retreat among Willows* suggests the tranquillity of such settings: two poets sitting in an airy room overlooking the hills, streams and forests beyond are, like the foliage of the willows that arc above them, literally and imaginarily opened up to the landscape.

If the willow is often an emblem of nature as muse in the East, it has also served as a figure of female beauty in Chinese literature since at least the Han Dynasty (206 BCE–220 CE). The trope flourished in what is often considered the 'golden age' of Chinese poetry, the Tang period (618–907). Various features of the body were subject to willowy analogy, but the willowy waist held pride of place in poems celebrating the beauty of courtesans. One of Liu Yuxi's 'Willow

Branch Songs' describes a rivalry between trees and women: 'In the days when they were first planted before the Calyx Tower, / They vied for thinness with the lovely waists on the upper floors.'[7]

The ideal eyebrow was shaped like a willow leaf, its curves lovingly traced by commentators, and a woman's pubic hair was 'in the depths of willow shade'.[8] The graceful movement of the entire body was also willowy. Li Shangyin, a ninth-century poet, considered the impression of fluidity more important than the details: 'Whether the willow can love or not, / Never a time it does not dance . . . The beauty which shakes a kingdom must reach all through the body: / Who comes only to view a willow's eyebrows?'[9] Similarly, in a poem on the dancing of her maidservant, Yang Yuhuan, consort of the Qing emperor Xuanzong and one of the 'four beauties' of ancient China, compared a dancing courtesan's alluring fragrance to that of a willow swaying in the wind: 'Gauzy sleeves release their scent . . . And a delicate pondside willow starts to brush the water, to sway.'[10]

As a symbol of spring, the willow was particularly suited to represent courtesans, who facilitated patrons' erotic awakenings and sated their 'willow feelings' (sexual desires).[11] Willow (*liu*) became a 'virtual trademark' for many in the capital cities who adopted the willow as part of their names or nicknames. Chang tai, the brothel area in Chang'an, was filled with 'Chang tai Willows'; to 'pluck a willow at Chang Terrace' was slang for visiting a prostitute, and elsewhere 'reposing beneath' or 'lying among willows' meant the same thing.[12] Many *ci* poems of the Tang period — verses set to popular brothel songs — employed the willow/woman trope. Composed by the 'willows' themselves as well as literati, however, they offer different perspectives on the analogy. In the mid-eighth century, Han Hung wrote to the courtesan Liu (willow),

Chang Terrace Willow
Chang Terrace Willow
Your beauty was so green and fresh, is it still thus?

Even though your long tendrils hang as before,
They must have been plucked by other men's hands.

Liu responds to this self-absorbed anxiety of possession with an account of the pain of being 'plucked' and abandoned:

Willow branch
In the fragrant and lovely season.
How hateful that year after year it is presented as a token
    of departure.
One leaf following the wind suddenly announces autumn;
Even though you come, how can I bear to be plucked?[13]

Another courtesan similarly laments her painful predicament:

Do not pluck me,
Plucking me is too unfair.
I'm a willow near the pond by the [Ou] River.
This man broke me, that man plucked me:
Each one's love lasted only a moment.[14]

The fate of older courtesans was to become 'faded willow'.[15] This sad image was literalized by Liu Yuxi in the next two lines of the poem quoted above, in which the women and willow have fully merged: 'Now . . . they lie abandoned in the long boulevards. / Whom would they mourn, these dew-laden leaves that seem to weep?'[16]

Implicit in the willow analogy, which relies on the stirring of the senses and the desire for union, is an intimation of inevitable future loss. In China, willow branches were often given at sorrowful partings, perhaps because *liu* sounds like a verb meaning to ask someone to stay.[17] Although such offerings were meant to 'bind friends' souls together', they did not ensure reunion.[18] The speaker in Zhou Dehua's ninth-century poem 'Willow Branches' recalls a long-ago enactment of this ritual: 'Along one bend of the river Clear, a thousand willow withies: twenty years past, on that old plank bridge, I parted from my love. No word from him, no news – this morning still no word.'[19] Images of such separations abound in farewell poems, sometimes with the whole landscape materializing the grief of parting. In one from 1087 by the Song Dynasty polymath Su Shi, willow flowers are literally wept: 'When you look closely, / These are not willow catkins, / But, drop after drop, parted lovers' tears!'[20]

The Japanese adopted the Chinese poetics of willows. In the *Kaifūsō*, an eighth-century collection of Chinese-style poetry, the willow appears more frequently than any other plant – even pine, bamboo and plum – as it does in Tang poetry.[21] In the refined world of the Heian court, exchanges of poems on coloured paper, often attached to artfully chosen branches or flowers, demonstrated the aesthetic sensibility of the writers. In *The Pillow Book*, the eleventh-century memoirs and musings of one of the Empress Teishi's ladies in waiting, Sei Shōnagon describes a 'letter on fine green paper, tied to a sprig of willow covered in little leaf buds' as a thing of 'elegant beauty'.[22] Later, willow became explicitly linked with poetry itself. Edo-period authors adopted willowy pseudonyms such as Ryūtei Tanehiko, 'Master of the Willow Pavilion', and Senryū Karai, 'River Willow', and the popular three-line poetic form named after the latter, *senryu*, was collected into canonical willowy anthologies: *Yanagidaru* (willow or willow sake barrel) and *Yanaginohazue* (willow leaf tips).[23]

As in Europe, willow was celebrated by the Japanese as a bridging figure, between seasons, for example: 'Snow is still falling in the mountains; willows are already blooming.'[24] Willows are not only temporal thresholds, however; they reveal that which cannot be seen, twining together the visible and invisible worlds, as a haiku by Saryū attests: 'Without a brush / The willow paints the wind.'[25] If willows heighten the sensual awareness of the viewer, they too respond empathetically to their environments. Yosa Buson, an eighteenth-century haiku poet, wrote, 'Plum flowers are all fallen. Willow trees will be sad for a while.'[26] As are humans who view in willows their mortal arboreal counterparts: 'the willow tree / by the lone teahouse – / it has grown old'.[27]

In Japan, as in China, willow was associated with the courtesan. In addition to the willow waist (*yanagigoshi*), the 'willow nose' (the word *hana* means both willow flowers and nose) and windblown 'willow hair' were celebrated. Willows were planted at the gates of brothel areas, called 'flower and willow towns' (*Karyukai*), and served not only as an intimation of the pleasures within but also as a border between the worlds of reality and fantasy. Those marking the edge of the red light district in Edo (Tokyo) were called 'looking-back willows' (*Mikaeri-yanagi*).[28] Frequently pictured in Japanese woodblock prints, these elegant sheltering trees frame scenes of parting and promises of future pleasures. Utagawa Hiroshige's print *The Willow Tree of Farewells* (1853, see pp. 142–3) depicts a group of revellers leaving the pleasure quarters. Shown out by girls bearing lanterns, they linger, already looking back with sweet regret.

The allure of willowy women has a darker side. There are various versions of the Japanese tale of Aoyagi, but they share the same basic plot: in the fifteenth century, a young samurai named Tomotada is sent on a mission by his lord. When a terrible snowstorm arises, he is relieved to stumble across a cottage beside which three willows grow. An old couple and a young girl with wild hair who live there shelter him for the night, over the course of which the samurai and the beautiful Aoyagi, whose name means green willow, exchange poetry and fall in love. Although a samurai may not marry without his lord's permission, Tomotada is so enamoured that he forgets his duty. The young lovers have several years of happiness, which come to an abrupt end when Aoyagi collapses and, just before she dies, confesses that she is the spirit of a willow tree. Travelling back to the old couple's cottage, the samurai finds nothing but three stumps.[29] A woodcut illustration by Bertha Lum poses Aoyagi in front of her tree, her face as white as the snow-covered ground, her robes the colour of blue shadow and the sinuous branches of the willow floating around her like windblown hair.

If in China and Japan willows are sensual, erotic and tinged with melancholy, these qualities are pushed to their extremes in the Persian

Bertha Lum, *Aoyagi*,
1907, woodblock
print, ink on paper.

tradition, where weeping willows (*Bid-i Majnun*) are mad. The Arabic word *majnun* means mad (crazy) or possessed, and in the case of *Bid-i Majnun*, links the tree to the love story of Laili and Majnun, an Arabic tale immortalized in the twelfth century by the Persian poet Nizami Ganjavi. In the poem, a poor Bedouin named Qays is passionately in love with, and loved in return by, the beautiful and privileged Laili. Her father forbids them to wed and forces Laili to marry a nobleman. Qays is literally driven mad, becoming *majnun*, and he wanders about the desert; Laili dies of a broken heart and later the body of her mad

Utagawa Hiroshige, *The Willow Tree of Farewells to Guests at Nihon Embankment in the New Yoshiwara*, from the series *Famous Places in Edo*, 1853, woodblock print, ink and colour on paper.

lover is found beside her grave.[30] The pendent boughs and shaking leaves of the *Bíd-i Majnun*, then, are those of a creature literally sick with love. And in Mughal miniatures, melancholy women are often pictured lost in reverie under the pendulous branches of willows (see p. 147).

In the West, the willow is also associated with the poetics of love, loss and descent into unreason. In Greek myth, Orpheus' poetic gift, so powerful he could charm even stones, was bound to willow. A lost fifth-century BCE painting by Polygnotus in the Temple of Apollo at Delphi included a depiction of the poet seated on a hill, holding 'a harp in his left hand, and in his right hand the leaves of a willow-tree' in a grove 'sacred to Persephone', according to Pausanias.[31] When Orpheus journeyed into Hades to bring back Eurydice, he carried willow branches. Although he failed in his quest, his descent into the underworld – or, as many critics have seen it, into the irrational world of the unconscious – was the wellspring of his poetry.

In his cycle *Sonnets to Orpheus* (1922), written as a 'grave-marker' for his daughter's recently deceased friend, Rainer Maria Rilke employed a deliberately topsy-turvy formulation to describe Orpheus' path to poetry: 'More expertly bends the willow branches / He who has experi-enced the willow's roots.'[32] In these two lines the willow first appears to bend its own branches, before we learn that it is in fact the poet who is the shaper; but if bending willow branches is the poet's art, the willow itself is also a poet who guides Orpheus' journey. By following the course of the willow's sinuous limbs from the depths of the soil to the aerial realm and back down to earth along its pendent boughs, the poet *becomes* willowy and thus capable of weaving willowy, pliable words into art.[33] The willow, which belongs to both the underworld and the world above, thus serves as a guide for the poet whose songs open up 'a passage from one realm to another',[34] showing the roots of life in death.

In Virgil's *Eclogues*, the first-century BCE Latin poems so central to the Western pastoral tradition, willows are ambivalent images. They frame scenes of love: 'my love and I would be together . . . among the willows, beneath the sheltering vines'. They also, however, mark the

boundary of belonging and exile. In the first eclogue a shepherd
who has been dispossessed of his lands (the future Emperor Augustus
having given them to a returning soldier) notices 'the hedge of willows
that marks / This the edge of what you own.' Having lost his own defin-
ing willow border, beneath whose flowers he will never again drowse,
he will 'sing [his] songs' no more. Willows, in the *Eclogues*, demarcate
the realm of love and poetry; outside their flowery threshold, there
is only loss.[35]

In Western poetry, forsaken lovers, when the 'rose' of love is dead,
are figured as wearing willow garlands 'bedew'd with teares'.[36] And in
Shakespeare, willows often stand for sorrow, whether that of parting, betrayal or death. In Act IV Scene 3 of *Othello*, shortly before
her murder at the hands of a husband who wrongly suspects her of
infidelity, Desdemona sings a song she learned from her mother's maid
who was also forsaken in love. 'An old thing 'twas', Desdemona tells her
maid Emilia, 'but it expressed her fortune, / And she died singing it.
That song tonight / Will not go from my mind.' While Emilia prattles,
Desdemona gives voice to her melancholy and rejection in the song,
which was also 'an old thing' to Elizabethan audiences:

> The poor soul sat sighing by a sycamore tree,
> 　　Sing all a green willow.
> Her hand on her bosom, her head on her knee,
> 　　Sing willow, willow, willow.
> The fresh streams ran by her and murmured her moans,
> 　　Sing willow, willow, willow.
> Her salt tears fell from her and softened the stones,
> 　　Sing willow, willow, willow.

The 'willow, willow, willow' refrain appears in sixteenth-century songs
and poems and was well known by the early seventeenth century, when
Othello was written. Printed song sheets record more verses than are
featured in the play, and other 'willow garland' ditties were also popu -
lar. Shakespeare played on the familiarity of the lyrics, having Desdemona

interrupt herself as she prepares for bed with a forgiving and self-critical Freudian slip: '"Sing all a green willow must be my garland. / Let nobody blame him; his scorn I approve" – / Nay, that's not next.' As familiarity becomes uncertainty we, like Desdemona, wonder, dread and deny what *is* next, and the next time we see her, in Act V Scene 2, Othello smothers her. The willow song returns when Emilia is murdered by her husband shortly thereafter. As she dies, she sings 'Willow, willow, willow' before telling Othello: 'Moor, she was chaste. She loved thee, cruel Moor.'

This scene has been deemed 'one of the most dramatically compelling' in Shakespeare's *oeuvre*, one of the playwright's 'most astonishing feats in dramaturgy'.[37] Precisely what makes it so powerful, however, is open to debate. In the Elizabethan period, the willow song was usually sung by men scorned by women. By assuming the part of the wronged lover in the song, Desdemona identifies with Othello, feels and understands his (imagined) betrayal. Perhaps, then, it is the poignant struggle between Desdemona's loyalty to and empathy for Othello on the one hand, and her own desire to live on the other, that makes the scene so charged. The repetition of the refrain leads Desdemona to her inexorable end, her interruptions – 'Nay, that's not next!' – futile and tension-heightening attempts to stay Othello's hand. But let us consider the repetition of the word 'willow' itself.

The often empty-sounding speech of Othello – the 'hollowness' of his 'orotundity',[38] in one critic's words – has been linked to the almost endless repetition in his lines of the letter 'O'; this vowel resounds insistently in the speech and names of the other characters as well. The Shakespeare scholar Joel Fineman famously argued that this omnipresent sound, this echoing 'O', materializes the hollowness not only of Othello but of all the play's characters, articulates the lack that makes each a desiring subject. Shakespeare derived the name Othello from the Greek *ethelō*, meaning desire, thus the *Tragedy of Othello* is the tragedy of desire itself, with Desdemona (from the Greek *dusdaimon*, unfortunate) proof that it can never be satisfied. Desire is not only articulated but created through language in the play; Desdemona

Mughal album leaf, 18th century.

is wooed by Othello's words, and the characters are developed, enunciated and undone through speech in which hollow 'O's in the form of apostrophes and groans as well as bits of bigger words abound. The willow scene is so 'profoundly strange and haunting', according to Fineman, in part because of its meta-theatrical significance, its undoing of Shakespeare's *author*-ity: the willow song, which is not by the playwright, marks his limits as a writer and as a subject of language; the repetition of the word 'willow' marks the author's self – Will – as always Othered with an 'O'. Indeed, the 'O' in willow calls to us all 'from an elsewhere that is other'.[39] Willow in *Othello*, then, is the signifier of the subject's constitution in language, of the subject who is hollow with desire.

The association of a hollowed-out subject and the vowel 'O' can be found elsewhere in Shakespeare's *oeuvre*. In Act III Scene I of *Hamlet*, Ophelia laments, 'O, woe is me'. This cry of a hollow self (O, O is me), like her name (O-philia), marks her as almost perversely open to others. Driven mad by her father's murder and Hamlet's insinuations of her harlotry, she drowns offstage. Gertrude describes her death in Act IV Scene 7:

There is a willow grows aslant a brook,
That shows his hoar leaves in the glassy stream.
Therewith fantastic garlands did she make
Of crow-flowers, nettles, daisies, and long purples,
That liberal shepherds give a grosser name,
But our cold maids do dead men's fingers call them.
There, on the pendent boughs her crownet weeds
Clamb'ring to hang, an envious sliver broke,
When down the weedy trophies and herself
Fell in the weeping brook. Her clothes spread wide,
And mermaid-like awhile they bore her up;
Which time she chanted snatches of old tunes,
As one incapable of her own distress,
Or like a creature native and endued

Unto that element. But long it could not be
Till that her garments, heavy with their drink,
Pulled the poor wretch from her melodious lay
To muddy death.

In this impossible speech – so full of naturalistic (and sexually charged) detail it seems there must have been an eyewitness who could have rescued Ophelia – the willow can be read as more than a vegetal prop. Showing 'his hoar leaves in the glassy stream', the willow may be seen as Hamlet's vegetable counterpart, showing his whore (Ophelia) leaves (garlands) and how to leave (by committing suicide) in the mirror below, before his 'envious sliver' causes her to fall into dissolution (her 'clothes spread wide') and death.

The play's suggestion that Ophelia's virtue, like her name and her self, is hollow was taken up by the Pre-Raphaelite painter John Everett Millais. His *Ophelia* (see overleaf) is now famous for the story of its making: posing for the painter in a bathtub heated by lamps, the model Elizabeth Siddal said nothing when the flames went out and the water grew icy cold. Millais did not notice, and she became ill and nearly died. The painting was notorious in its own day, however, for the way Ophelia was depicted, with arms and lips provocatively parted, floating beneath a fallen willow. In a period when prostitutes and fallen women often drowned themselves in the Thames, Millais's work was widely considered too transgressive a vision of Shakespeare's 'love-lorn maiden', whom critics were shocked to see 'souse[d]' in a 'weedy ditch'.[40]

In Shakespeare's plays the willowy, desiring subject is not always fated to tragedy. In Act 1 Scene 5 of *Twelfth Night*, Viola, disguised as Cesario, is sent by Orsino to court the reluctant Olivia on his behalf. In answer to Olivia's question what would s/he do to woo her, Viola/Cesario replies,

Make me a willow cabin at your gate
And call upon my soul within the house,

Sir John Everett Millais, *Ophelia*, 1851–2, oil on canvas.

> Write loyal cantons of contemnèd love,
> And sing them loud even in the dead of night;
> Halloo your name to the reverberate hills,
> And make the babbling gossip of the air
> Cry out 'Olivia!' O, you should not rest
> Between the elements of air and earth
> But you should pity me.

In this beautiful passage, the whole world becomes a soundbox for the lover's lamentations and longing – reverberate hills and gossip of the air echoing the call of love unceasingly. Viola/Cesario presents a willowy model of subjectivity similar to that proposed in *Othello*: the lover's soul is not within him or her, but is an absent core always somewhere else, in someone else's house; the state of desire is always one on the willowy margins, calling out for recognition. In the play the would-be lovers are rife with 'O's and otherness (Olivia loves Cesario who is Viola in disguise who loves Orsino); the elusive erotics of poetic language and the eternally ungraspable object of desire are suggested by all these 'O's.

The elusive but haunting beloved is also explored in Dante Gabriel Rossetti's 'Willowwood' poems of 1868, which imagine a lover in mourning. The first sonnet begins, 'I sat with Love upon a woodside well, / Leaning across the water, I and he.' The couple stare, Narcissus-like, into the mirroring pool, and Love begins to play his lute. The lover's tears upset the image, transforming Love's reflected visage into an unnamed 'hers' (the lover, this conflation suggests, is as much in love with love as with his lost lady). Love excites the waters further with his wings, so that as the lover stoops, 'her own lips rising there / Bubbled with brimming kisses at my mouth.' In the second poem, Love sings, and the lover becomes aware of a 'dumb throng, / That stood aloof, one form by every tree, / All mournful forms, for each was I or she, / The shades of those our days that had no tongue.' In Sonnet 3, Love addresses this forest of shadowy memories, of wander-ing souls bound to willows depicted so ethereally by Margaret

Macdonald Mackintosh: 'O ye, all ye that walk in Willowwood, / That walk with hollow faces burning white' and are imprisoned in a love-haunted 'lifelong night'. Would it not be better, Love asks, to forget and be forgotten:

> Alas! The bitter banks in Willowwood,
> With tear-spurge wan, with blood-wort burning red:
> Alas! If ever such a pillow could
> Steep the soul in sleep till she were dead, –
> Better all life forget her than this thing,
> That Willowwood should hold her wandering!

In the final sonnet, the lover, who has been embracing the watery image of his beloved, lets 'the kiss unclose; / And her face fell back drowned, and was as grey / As its grey eyes.' He then leans low and like a vampire drinks 'A long draught of water where she sank, / Her breath and all her tears and all her soul'; and Love pities and embraces him.[41]

The sonnets are full of sound repetitions, 'W's, 'L's, and 'O's in particular, that fill the imaginary woods with the haunting echoes of half-remembered wooing. The labial sounds of many of the lines – the 'P's, 'B's, 'M's, 'W's and other letters that require the reader to close the lips partly or completely – sensually but solitarily re-enact the lovers' kisses. Yet the poems also have a sinister air, less in their invocation of the dead than in the wished-for violence of forgetting, imagined as a kind of drowning or smothering by a willowbank pillow that might 'steep the soul in sleep till she were dead'. The literary scholar Isobel Armstrong has argued that the 'liquid "l" consonant' that 'saturates' virtually every line of the four sonnets creates a sense of the poem itself as 'afloat in the medium of these liquid sounds'. Lover, beloved and even reader are thus sonically tempted with 'dissolution', with the lure of the unconscious immersion that would quench the desire that keeps the faces of those who walk in Willowwood 'burning white'. The sonnet form, though, keeps in check the 'structurelessness of water and ripple', and the lover can push away the grey face, devour her (after)life so he can be free.[42]

The Willowwood poems are often thought to be a form of visionary autobiography, in which Rossetti describes his haunting by Elizabeth Siddal. Lizzie, his wife, had died of a laudanum overdose in 1862; whether her death was suicide or accidental is unknown, but the poet, who had been unfaithful to her, had much to regret. He had begun a relationship with William Morris's wife Jane some time before the sonnets were written, but despite the lover's pushing her away in the sonnets, Lizzie's spectre refused to be exorcized. Rossetti had her body exhumed just over nine months after he wrote the Willowwood sonnets so that he could retrieve the manuscript of some poems he had buried with her, as though trying to rescue his poetic self from the depths of her tomb – to regain the 'tongue' the lover in the sonnets has lost. Afterwards, however, the memory of the willowy, lonely Lizzie – associated with water and willow since at least 1851, when Millais painted her as Ophelia – still lingered.

In Rossetti's painting *Water Willow* (1871), Lizzie's absence, symbolized by the *Salix* branches that fill the foreground, literally frames Rossetti's vision of Jane Morris. The pair were then living at Kelmscott Manor, visible in the upper left of the canvas. While the recognizable landscape background, unusual for Rossetti, suggests that the artist wanted to anchor Jane in a particular time and place, her face, with its enormous eyes and sensual lips, appears against the water like an after-image of the beloved's face in the Willowwood sonnets. The figure slips from the present in other ways too: Jane's dark cloud of hair seems buoyant, floating, and her deep robes sink into the willowy, watery landscape, for although we view the distant house straight on, we view the figure from above. The shadow of death touches Jane in the shape of a sickle at the base of her long neck and, most curiously, in the hand that holds the willow at lower right, which can read as Jane's own but also appears as the hand of another, invisible but palpable presence, who can show her how to 'wear the willow'. Shortly after this painting was made, William Morris began to design

Dante Gabriel Rossetti, *Water Willow*, 1871, oil on canvas glued onto wood panel.

his willow-patterned wallpapers, which may now be seen in a more melancholy light.

Christina Rossetti took up the Willowwood refrain in 'An Echo from Willowwood', a poem of 1870 that addresses the narcissism of her brother's vision. The title, sounds, sonnet form and epigraph ('O ye, all ye that walk in Willowwood') of her poem echo Dante's, but Christina refuses to drown Narcissus' female lover, Echo, and offers an account of the shared grief of lovers who must part: 'Two gazed into a pool', not lover and Love, but 'he' and 'she'. On the brink of the water and of parting, both lovers experience grief: 'Each tasted bitterness which both must drink.' At last a ripple, not caused by Love's upset but by something in the outer world, shatters the vision of lovers joined, 'So those hearts joined . . . were parted so.'[43] Marking a break from the Victorian romanticization of willow-haunting and -haunted lovers, W. H. Auden's poem 'Underneath an Abject Willow' of 1936 urges the lonely figure sitting beneath it – Benjamin Britten, to whom the poem is dedicated and who set it to music – to 'sulk no more', to leave the willow and its associations behind: 'Stand up and fold / Your map of desolation . . . Walk then, come / No longer numb / Into your satisfaction.'[44] Other writers in a variety of genres, however, have suggested how difficult it is to escape the willow's hold over lovers and others.

Hans Christian Andersen's fairy tale 'Under the Willow Tree' of 1853 is a story of unrequited love, in which the willow metamorphoses from a figure of the carefree world of childhood into an emblem of isolation and death. When the self-exiled protagonist learns of his love's impending marriage, he tries to return home. As he makes his weary night-time journey through freezing weather, he sits beneath a large willow tree by the side of the road and feels its branches engulf and embrace him like a father. He imagines the willow carrying him home to his childhood garden, where his beloved's icy indifference is thawed by his 'great love'; her tears burn his face and it is the 'loveliest moment of his life'. The willow weds fire and ice, father and mother, home and exile in this sublime dream, but it is an impossible one – the next morning he is found frozen to death.[45]

The potential horror of the willowy embrace was explored by Algernon Blackwood in 'The Willows', which H. P. Lovecraft considered the 'greatest weird tale ever written'.[46] First published in 1907, the short story is the haunting tale of an encounter with abso-lute otherness and death in the form of wild willows. Two friends who have embarked on a boat trip along the Danube find themselves, somewhere between Vienna and Budapest, in a landscape that has become unsettlingly indeterminate, a swampy zone 'covered by a vast sea of low willow-bushes' in which earth, water and vegetation blur. In this shifty region leaves rather than water form waves, and the islands themselves change with the flow of the water in a bewildering fashion. Destabilized and adrift in this strange place without reliable landmarks, the companions stop at the ephemeral islands only with difficulty: 'the willow branches tore our hands as we seized them to stop'. The ambiguity of the ubiquitous willows is felt at once: they rip the travellers' flesh but they also seem to clap 'their thousand little hands as though to applaud the success of [their] efforts'. Uncannily animate, they laugh, hum, shriek, cry, shake 'their big bushy heads' and twirl 'their myriad leaves even when there [is] no wind'. One of the islands on which the friends camp is the setting for a series of horrifying discoveries, and the narrator's friend suggests the willows have a fate worse than death in store for them: 'a radical alteration, a complete change, a horrible loss of oneself'. The experience of living nature radically transforms the narrator's understanding of the landscape and 'the standard of reality' itself. The titular willows, then, serve as disquieting emblems of non-human life and the birth of a new and different consciousness.[47]

In J.R.R. Tolkien's *The Lord of the Rings*, first published in 1954–5, a willowy encounter is also a catalyst for learning to recognize and respect living nature. In *The Fellowship of the Ring*, the hobbits journey through the labyrinthine Old Forest. When they reach the Withywindle valley, they find the dark river whose name links it to the willow and entanglement (withy means willow wand, and withywind is a type of twining convolvulus or bindweed) 'bordered with ancient willows, arched over with willows, blocked with fallen willows, and flecked with thousands of faded willow leaves'. Drawn to the shade of a particularly hoary old tree, Merry and Pippin are lulled to sleep by the faint music of its boughs. Sam hears a splash and 'a noise like the snick of a lock when a door quietly closes fast' and finds Frodo in the water, a willow root holding him down, Pippin vanished into the tree and Merry's upper half trapped inside the trunk. Rescue arrives when Tom Bombadil comes striding through the forest singing, 'Hey dol! merry dol! ring a dong dillo! / Ring a dong! hop along! fal lal the willow! . . . Poor old Willow-man, you tuck your roots away!' He sings his willow refrain into a crack in the siren-like tree, which releases Merry and Pippin from its snares.[48]

Tom brings the hobbits home with him and tells them about Old Man Willow, a 'mighty singer' whose 'cunning mazes' are difficult to escape. The hobbits learn of the 'hearts of trees and their thoughts', which are 'often dark and strange, and filled with a hatred of things that go free upon the earth, gnawing, biting, breaking, hacking, burning: destroyers and usurpers'. While Old Man Willow first appears a villain, however, it becomes increasingly difficult to condemn him. As the hobbits and the reader learn of the destruction that Saruman's orcs at Fangorn are wreaking on the forest, the hobbits' own land-clearing in the shire and policing of the bounds of the Old Forest are put into a new perspective – that of an ongoing and irresolvable struggle between the forces of wilderness and civilization.[49]

In J. K. Rowling's Harry Potter series, the whomping willow, like Tolkien's Old Man Willow, at first appears a malicious creature. This dangerous tree with branches 'thick as a python' is introduced in book two, when Ron and Harry crash a stolen, flying car into its boughs and it responds by attacking the unwanted intruder in its airy lair, 'its gnarled boughs' – pollarded ones like huge clubs in the film version – 'pummelling every inch of the car it could reach'. The reader learns that the willow is a valuable tree, though not why, and Professor Sprout tends to its wounds, putting several of its branches in slings.[50] Book three reveals that the willow was planted the year Remus Lupin came to Hogwarts, to stand as the sylvan guardian of his secret: at the full moon he follows the secret passage concealed beneath the willow's roots to the Shrieking Shack and there transforms into a werewolf. The willow's 'twigs clenched like knuckles' and 'vicious, swishing branches' protect others from harm and Lupin from discovery and the banishment that would result.[51] The violent tree is thus benevolent at root (where its 'off-button' is located). Unsurprisingly, the wand of Lily Evans (Harry's mother), which allows Harry to live, is made of willow.

It has been argued that the whomping willow functions, like the American Liberty Tree (a Boston rallying point for the revolutionaries) and the French revolution's *arbres de la liberté*, as an emblem of liberal politics and resistance to oppressive regimes. Over the course of the series Harry, Hermione and Ron encounter many instances of social and political injustice, from the slavery of house-elves to Sirius Black's being sentenced without trial to lifelong imprisonment at Azkaban. Harry and his friends free various subjugated creatures and fight government corruption. Magic cannot create a just society, and Rowling rejects the 'false positivism' offered by the control over nature that magic or science affords, proposing instead a positivism 'built on the ideals of the English Jacobins'.[52] The whomping willow thus enables Harry to learn of his own great injustice to Severus Snape, when he follows the passage to the Shrieking Shack during the Battle of Hogwarts in the final book and witnesses the murder of his seeming persecutor, who is revealed, in the memories Harry gathers from Snape in his dying moments, to be his lifelong protector.

One of the most memorable willow-sheltered revelations in literature occurs in Kenneth Grahame's *The Wind in the Willows*, which also enshrines a yearning for liberty. First published in 1908, the book was originally entitled *The Wind in the Reeds*, alluding to the music made by the Greek demi-god Pan on his rustic pipes. A collection of Yeats poems, however, had been published with a similar title in 1899, so Grahame's publisher proposed changing it to *The Wind in the Willows*, which had, he thought, 'a charming & wet sound'.[53] The wind in the willows is linked in the book not only with poetic inspiration but also with other kinds of sensual and aesthetic awakenings. The story begins with Mole heeding the call of spring and venturing out from his earthy lair to discover Rat and life on the river, and this pattern of call and response is repeated in each chapter. Overtly modelled on *The Odyssey* (the twelve-part book ends with a chapter called 'The Return of Ulysses'), *The Wind in the Willows* is a book of journeys and their consequences, which propel the characters through states of desire, intoxication, happiness, loss and grief. Many of these adventures take place along the river, above whose spiled banks gnarled, pollarded willows converse in Arthur Rackham's illustrations, spirits of the shoreline overseeing the lives of the little animals below them.

The central episode of the book occurs in chapter Seven, 'The Piper at the Gates of Dawn'. When Otter's son Portly goes missing, Mole and Rat set off to search for him. As they boat along the river, Rat begins to hear an intoxicating melody, though Mole at first only catches 'the wind playing the reeds and rushes and osiers'. The sound, which arouses a sense of longing 'that is pain', draws them to a small island 'fringed close with willow' just above a weir; they immediately sense it is 'full of significance', hiding 'whatever it might hold behind a veil'. Mooring their boat at the island's 'flowery margin', they push through the undergrowth and find themselves in a wild orchard. In this pagan grove they discover, to their awe, the god Pan in all his hairy, horned, wild glory, who is sheltering the sleeping Portly.

Arthur Rackham, chapter head for 'The River Bank' in Kenneth Grahame, *The Wind in the Willows* (London, 1940).

W. Graham
Robertson, cover of
Kenneth Grahame,
The Wind in the Willows
(London, 1908).

Pan blesses them with forgetting, though, so they do not live full of
regret for the dream of beauty and happiness they shared in his presence.[54] The cover of the 1908 edition, designed by W. Graham Robertson,
captures the spirit of this scene and the book: Mole and Rat have drawn
up in front of Pan's island (here fringed with water willow) and are
bowed in humble submission below the comparatively giant musical
god, enjoying a moment of sacred stillness in a book based around
the ever-moving river and the transience of all things.

The Wind in the Willows conflates a search for homecoming with
nature and the freedom to explore or escape. A quest for homecoming is similarly envisioned through the figure of the willow in the
penultimate novel of Hubert Selby Jr, author of *Last Exit to Brooklyn*
and *Requiem for a Dream*. In *The Willow Tree* (1998), Bobby, an African
American teenager, and his Hispanic girlfriend Maria are attacked while
walking down the street by a Hispanic gang who dislike interracial
mingling. They throw acid in Maria's face and beat Bobby severely.
After crawling into an abandoned basement, Bobby is rescued by an
old holocaust survivor, the benevolent Moishe, who nurses him back to

health. Maria, however, commits suicide while she is in hospital. Moishe takes Bobby several times to Prospect Park while he is recuperating, to sit under a willow tree that reminds the old man of one he and his wife and son used to visit before they were captured by the Nazis and taken to a concentration camp. By the side and with the help of the figure of the willow tree, Moishe, the sole survivor in his family, works through his grief and desire for revenge and is able to move beyond racial and cultural prejudice. For Bobby too, the tree becomes an image simultaneously of loss, mourning and hope. Moishe's 'family tree' comes to include Bobby, and the willow offers a vision of an open, ramifying structure that does not exclude or forget the past but symbolizes a less violent future.[55]

The legacy of the Second World War is also treated through the image of a willow tree in Carolyn Forché's poem 'The Garden Shukkei-en'. The narrator and a Hiroshima survivor who had been in the titular garden when the nuclear bomb was dropped walk through the restored grounds, crossing by way of 'a vanished bridge' into a world where past and present can never be dissociated. The woman recalls how her skin 'hung from [her] fingertips like cloth' and does not like a red flower that reminds her 'of a woman's brain crushed under a roof'. In the tranquillity of the garden, the river teems with memories of 'the living / and the dead both crying for help', and a weeping willow 'etches its memory of their faces into the water'. The violent means of this mark-making (etchings are made with acid) infuses the waters that could not cool the victims' burns. Even though where 'light touches the face, the character for heart is written', it remains largely forgotten 'in the silence surrounding what happened to us'.[56] The willow in the garden, though, witness to unimaginable horrors, never stops inscribing its remembrance, which, if recognized, might teach us how to be human.

We will conclude our look at willow literature with a brief consideration of a text in which the author meditates on the material conditions of writing, mortality and hope for the future. Shortly before he died in 1922, the Russian Futurist poet Velimir Khlebnikov composed a short essay entitled 'The Willow Twig', dated 'Willow Sunday' (Palm Sunday) and subtitled 'Tools of the Writer's Trade'. The text begins,

> I am writing at this very moment with a twig cut from a dried branch of pussy willow; little puffs of silvery down still cling to it, like puffy rabbits who have come out to contemplate the springtime. They cover the dry black twig on every side.

As these musing Easter bunnies animating the writing instrument perhaps already suggest, the essay is intended 'as a different glance at the infinite, at the "nameless," a different way of seeing things'. The explicit pretext for the text is news the poet has received relating to his recent experience in Iran as part of a Soviet attempt to back up a rebellion against the Shah: Kuchuk-khan (1880–1921), the rebel who had, for a time, the support of the Russians, betrayed his compatriots and, under attack, retreated to the Iranian mountains where he froze to death in a blizzard. Shah loyalists decapitated him and sent the head to Tehran. Kuchuk-khan's death inspires Khlebnikov's effort to *see* differently, but this attempt is inseparable from his practice of *writing* differently: he mentions three woody instruments he has recently used to write with – the 'harsh quill of a forest porcupine' in Iran and a blackthorn spine in addition to the pussy willow pen – all of which frame and inscribe the moment of his writing as well as the revolutionary events the essay describes. Kuchuk-khan, the author tells us, 'fled to the mountains, there to behold death in the form of snow'; there his life 'came to a snowy full stop'. The essay thus conflates writing and the real – death equals punctuation (a 'full stop') – through inversion of expectations (full stops are usually not white).

For the previous decade Khlebnikov had been attempting to create a universal poetic language which would transcend reason and open up a cosmic dimension of experience by freeing words from their conventional meanings and functions. In 'The Willow Twig', the new consciousness the poet wanted to inspire is suggested, and perhaps even

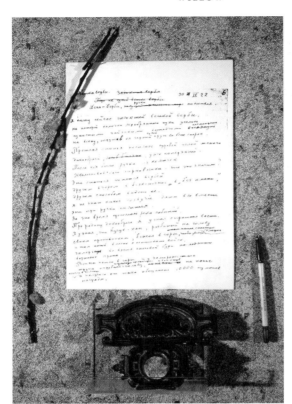

Khlebnikov's pussy
willow pen.

created, by the paradoxical conflations of the text. The whiteness of
snow and death becomes indistinguishable from that of catkins and
bunnies, symbols of spring and life, just as the writing instrument
and the text merge oneirically – the black line of the dried twig inter-
rupted by its white catkins echoing as much as inscribing the black line
and white spaces of Khlebnikov's text. The essay ends with what at
first seems like a flippant remark: 'But in the heaven of that period's
events, the most powerful star was Miturich's Easter sculpture made of
cheesecake, "Faith in Four Dimensions".' Khlebnikov associated poetic
consciousness with hyperspace; here the four-sided, pyramidal Easter
cheesecake made by his artist friend Petr Miturich and inscribed with
the symbols of different faiths – a white tomb, a star against the
blackness of space (another white 'full stop') made to celebrate the

end of Lent and the fertility of spring – expands the two dimensions of linear twig and text into universal volume and cyclical time. The revolution of catkins around the twig, Kuchuk-khan's failed political revolution, the revolution of the seasons and the stars, and the poet's desired revolution of consciousness are thus brought together in the open closing of Khlebnikov's essay.[57]

five

Brushes with Fame

❦

S ome of the greatest artists from East and West have been drawn to willow, as much for its lines, whether sinuous or spiky, and varied palette as for its cultural significance. More than simply a recurring motif, though, willow is intimately associated with the production of art. The best charcoal is made from it, and its wood has also been used for the stems and handles of paintbrushes. In recent decades it has become a favourite material of environmental artists and for living sculptures. More abstractly, depictions of pollard willows, with their sprays of wands, often resemble bristly paintbrushes, while the winding tresses of pendent branches evoke the dynamic line of ink brushwork. This chapter will examine how artists have used willow in a variety of media as a way of commenting on their time and their artistic projects.

In Chinese landscape painting, willow expressed a wide variety of meanings and was open to many styles of rendering. In previous chapters we have encountered Gong Xian's stunted, wild willows as a symbol of exile and the serenity of Zhao Lingrang's willowy scholar's retreat, but the work of Ma Yuan, the foremost Southern Song dynasty painter, offers us one of the most sophisticated artistic treatments of willow. In the late twelfth century he became renowned for compositions 'leaning on one corner'.[1] In these, juxtaposed fragments, contrasts of calligraphic brushwork and gentle washes, extremes of near and far and distortions of scale and form work to create emotively evocative scenes.[2] In *Bare Willows and Distant Mountains*, the impossibly tall and elegantly brushed titular willows frame the characteristic one-corner composition and offer a model of seeing that bridges spans of time as well as space.

This ink painting on silk depicts a landscape in early spring, when the willows are still bare but the plum trees have started to bud, in the stillness of the early morning, when water, mist and branches are undisturbed. At the bottom right, a tiny traveller on foot, perhaps a servant once following his mounted lord (the silk immediately to his left is damaged so it is impossible to tell), approaches two slender willows that stand like pillars at the entrance to the vast and airy landscape beyond, a landscape that becomes progressively less solid, more veiled in mist and fantasy, as one's eye travels into the distance. The viewer, like the traveller, is poised before an open-ended prospect.

Ma Yuan, *Bare Willows and Distant Mountains*, end of 12th century (Southern Song Dynasty), ink and colour on silk, round fan mounted as an album leaf.

167

Though unmoving, the inclined and arcing willows trace a path through the expansive space. The trunk of the closer one leans heavily to the left, directly towards the foot of the bridge, to which a number of daintily trailing fronds of both willows point. The leftmost branches gesture towards the mist-shrouded village, while the gentle curves of others echo the contour of the opposite river-bank that winds away to the invisible feet of the distant mountains, whose rounded shoulders seem to rest on nothing but air. The further willow leads us, via an ascending series of rounded branches, like foothills, first to the top of the lowest mountain at the right and finally, with a formal echo, to the tallest mountain in the distance on the left, whose bumpy peaks are mimicked by the outline of the willow's topmost bending branches in a subtle 'interweave' of close-ness and distance.[3] Another formal echo returns us from the furthest peak to the closest point of the foreground: the pale blue with which the mountain silhouette is faintly washed is picked up, in this near-monochrome work, by the dotted buds of the plum tree branch at bottom centre.

If the two willows literally inscribe an imaginary journey of discovery and bridge foreground and distance, they do so not only through the vectors of their lines but also through their varied brush-work. The thick, firmly rooted trunks, outlined and subtly shaded to suggest volume, give way, as they ascend, to single lines of liquid ink like 'spraying fountain[s]' sending 'arcs of fronds' into the sky, in the words of the art historian Richard Edwards.[4] They figure the literally transformational possibilities of the voyage, from here to somewhere else, from reality to pure, as yet obscure, formal possibility, of which we can see only the barest outline. The willow thus embodies the dynamism of the brush itself. The implicit metamorphoses of tree and style are temporal as well as spatial: when the traveller reaches the distant mountains, their pale spectres, like the willow branches, will have taken on life and character. As another art historian put it, Ma Yuan's leafless willows cause us 'to hold our breath in expectation of that imminent burst of springtime green'.[5]

Bare Willows and Distant Mountains, then, is 'a painting of promise, of beginnings',[6] in which the willow embodies a vision of becoming, of a future yet to be seen. It is also nostalgic for the past: after the Song lost control of northern China to the Jin, they moved their capital into their southern territories, and the monumental paintings of the Northern Song gave way to the smaller paintings of Ma Yuan's period, the format and subjects of which suggest introspection and a yearning for lost spaces. Metaphorically, and more urbanely, the painting offers another willowy 'interweave' of near and far: painted fans like this were avidly collected and pasted into albums in the Song period.[7] As we know, feminine beauty was frequently likened to that of the willow. The intimate female proximity suggested by the form of the fan – along with connotations of courtly ritual, social activity and the enclosed world of the city – forms a piquant contrast to the painting's vision of a solitary male (or a master and servant) travelling through an infinitely open landscape. This pleasing disparity is simultaneously activated and bridged by imagining the movement of the fan stirring both the air around it and the branches of the willow, setting the tranquil scene in motion. Ma Yuan's painting can thus be seen as a medium-specific meditation on various sorts of willowy pleasures, interplays and prospects. His willows, like the painter himself (whose name, Yuan, means 'distance'), are facilitators of imaginary journeys.

In the centuries after Ma Yuan, willows remained popular motifs in Chinese art. A seventeenth-century painting manual extols their beauty by comparing weeping willows that have been recently cropped to 'a young girl whose hair has been trimmed in a fringe on her brow. Their slender grace is beyond words.'[8] Gong Xian wrote in his *Secrets of Painting* that 'if you carry in your mind any preconceptions at all about painted willows, then you can never succeed' at painting them.[9] Despite this warning, manuals offered both interpretive glosses and instruction on the trees' rendering. *The Mustard Seed Garden Manual of Painting*, named after the garden of its publisher, is a technical treatise on landscape painting. First published in 1679, it became a standard teaching text

Wang Gai et al., *Jie zi yuan hua zhuan* (The Mustard Seed Garden Manual of Painting), 19th-century edition.

for later artists, and in the section on trees, it lists four methods of painting willows:

> The first is to outline and fill in with green. The second is to use a light, fresh green to draw in new shoots, a fresh yellow for the tips of new leaves, and a dark green for shadows and accents. The third method is to add a dark green to the light-green dotting first applied, and to touch up with ink some of the parts where the green has been applied. Lastly, some parts

Utagawa Hiroshige, *Yatsumi Bridge*, from the series *One Hundred Famous Views of Edo*, 1856, woodblock print, ink on paper.

may be left with only a few fine ink strokes and a bit more dotting in dark green.

Varying degrees of ink outline, shading and direct colour application distinguish the four methods, artists of different periods preferring different styles (Song painters 'usually dotted in the leaves' and painted willows 'tall with dripping foliage').[10] *The Mustard Seed Garden Manual* was illustrated with woodblock prints, but these could only partly, and diagrammatically, convey the text's ideas. A nineteenth-century edition, for example, illustrates a willow-fringed retreat. The willow branches are depicted hanging down in a somewhat stiff manner, and the foliage is indicated with a solid, largely unmodulated block of green also used for the ground. It was not until the nineteenth century that woodblock prints of willows could compete with paintings as treasured works of art in the East.

Japanese *ukiyo-e* or 'pictures of the floating world' were woodblock prints primarily produced for the common people in Edo (Tokyo), the administrative capital of the empire, from the seventeenth century onwards. Characterized by flat, bright colours, remarkable suggestions of light and atmosphere, and dramatic compositions in a hybrid style making use of Western perspective and Japanese outline drawing, the prints were produced in the thousands. Celebrations of the transient and mundane, they depict famous actors and courtesans, views of the modern city, tourist sites and other fleeting subjects. These mass-produced and widely circulated images were meant to be as ephemeral as the 'floating world' they depicted, but the sophistication and beauty of the best prints are timeless. The international influence of their style and subject matter, moreover, was profound, especially on the Impressionist painters who avidly collected them.

In his lifetime, Utagawa Hiroshige, one of the most accomplished *ukiyo-e* artists, designed thousands of colour woodblock prints in which the motif of the willow recurs over and over again. *Yatsumi Bridge* of 1856, part of a series of *One Hundred Famous Views of Edo*, is a typical example of both Hiroshige's *oeuvre* and the Japanese woodblock print tradition. In this daring composition, the pendent fronds of a willow tree hang as a partial screen over the view from one of the busy bridges in Edo. The umbrellas of the bustling passers-by and the dramatically arcing handrail of the bridge at the lower left, the fishing boats and poling men on a boat transporting fuel, and the two soaring birds suggest movement, labour and transient life. At the same time, the literally floating implied viewpoint, the stillness of Mount Fuji and the waters, and the horizontal horizon line convey calm stasis. The tiniest hint of movement in the willow's foliage reconciles the two 'moods' of the print: busy modern life and serene nature poetry. The leafy screen also serves to highlight the transparent clarity of the scene's light and atmosphere, which is in part achieved through the use of Prussian blue in the water and upper sky, and the technique of *bokashi*, wherein the ink applied to the block is partially wiped off to create transitions and a sense of translucence, visible here in the graduation from dark to light blue, and from red light over the horizon to the colour of the paper.

The movement of willows is much more dramatically captured in a work that is commonly considered not only Hiroshige's finest landscape but also the most beautiful print in his entire *oeuvre*. *Seba, the Thirty-Second Station* of c. 1840 is from the series *The Sixty-Nine Stations of the Kisokaidō Road*, depicting travellers' stops on the Kiso road connecting Edo and Kyoto. Tourism was increasingly popular in the period, and prints such as this one functioned as souvenirs as well as inducements to explore, imaginarily if not actually, the Japanese landscape. In the print, two boaters pole along the river Narai in the early evening, heading towards the station whose thatched roofs are visible along the horizon line.[11] Wind shapes the willows into claws reaching over the choppy waters, and a sense of struggle is expressed in the leaning trunks and the angle of the shoreline, boats and bodies, counterbalanced by the stubborn push of the slender poles. Night, indicated by the black *bokashi* at the top of the print, is beginning to fall, and the grain of the block showing through in the sky adds a glowering quality to the air. At the same time, the bright full moon, the fading orange clouds of sunset at the right and the luminous, nearly phosphorescent waters of the river irradiate the scene, creating a sense of harmony. The buffeted willow branches, dotted with agitated foliage, drop down peacefully in front of the moon's orb, which floats between the two clusters of buildings, and the ruffled waters of the foreground calm as they approach the station. Most of the prints in the series depict dusk and evening scenes; this one creates an astonishing sense both of a galvanizing elemental experience and of imminent repose, transient states (as fleeting as ephemeral woodblock prints) and eternal returns, extremes echoed in the form of the willows.

A beautiful Mughal miniature by Aqa Riza, a Persian artist who travelled to India and was adopted by the artistically inclined Prince Salim (who would become Emperor Jahangir in 1605), similarly captures something of the haunting poetry of the willow by framing a scene in which East and West, near and far, meet. The miniature reflects the painter's Persian origins in its delicate, calligraphic style and gorgeous colours, the motif of the weeping willow, and the Safavid chair. The more naturalistic face of the elegant musician, on the other

Utagawa Hiroshige, *Seba, the Thirty-Second Station*, from the series *The Sixty-Nine Stations of the Kisokaidō Road*, c. 1840, woodblock print.

Aqa Riza, *An Elegant Man Seated under a Willow Tree*, 1600–05, opaque watercolour and gold on paper.

hand, was a response to the European-influenced style embraced by the Mughal court.[12] Like the figure's feet and slippers, the trunk of the weeping willow is highly stylized, especially where it meets the rocky ground, but its lines become more fluid as they ascend, and the cascades of delicate foliage raining down are both naturalistic *and* patterned, as they are in life. The ambiguous veil they create screens the young man with the faraway look, who is simultaneously close and distant, while serving as a stylistic threshold between the arts of Europe and the Middle East.

The motif of the willow often served as a means of commenting on the relationship between art and nature in the West. While Eastern artists in general preferred the form of weeping willows, pollards occupied a central place in many Western artists' *oeuvres*. Somewhat surprisingly, William Gilpin, the eighteenth-century theorist of the picturesque in painting – all that is delightfully ramshackle, slightly wild but not frighteningly sublime – considered the weeping willow 'the only one of its tribe that is beautiful'.[13] A number of nineteenth-century authors concurred, declaring pollarded willows 'disagreeable to the eye of the painter', their 'decapitated trunks' presenting an 'unsightly spectacle'.[14] Despite this condemnation, however, artists from the Baroque to the modern periods have celebrated the aged trunks and vigorous new shoots of pollards. Vincent van Gogh wrote to his brother that if 'one draws a pollard willow as though it were a living being, which it actually is, then the surroundings follow more or less naturally'; the artist simply needs to 'rest' on the willow until there is 'some life in it'.[15] Dwelling on and with the willow for a time, the artist draws (on) its inner animation to fill in a world.

In *St Jerome Beside a Pollard Willow*, an etching with drypoint from 1648, Rembrandt used the pollard to comment on the production of his art and its relationship with nature and spirituality. The hoary, gnarled and broken trunk of the tree is the focus of the print, rising from a grassy knoll in the bottom left foreground to shield the mouth of a cave where a bespectacled St Jerome pursues his studies, accompanied by his lion, whose head peeks out from behind the trunk on the left. The composition is typical of a set of Rembrandt's etchings that are divided into two parts: a dominant motif from nature (the tree) and a subordinate symbolic scene (St Jerome in his hermitage), each subject to a different graphic treatment that demonstrates Rembrandt's technical virtuosity as a printmaker. The heavily worked tree is rich and velvety in tone, conveying a palpable substance and reality, whereas the surrounding scene has been lightly and rapidly sketched in; one gets a sense of the speed in the hastily scribbled lines that make up Jerome's shadow on the cave wall.

Rembrandt van Rijn, *St Jerome Beside a Pollard Willow*, 1648, etching with drypoint.

In Northern European art, Jerome was often represented with a
pollard willow or tree stump, sometimes shown turning away from
the dead tree to a crucifix, a godly 'tree' symbolizing the promise
of eternal rather than transient earthly life. Here, in an inversion of
the relative importance of the subjects, St Jerome is accorded less
weight than the pollard. Indeed, he serves primarily to highlight the

spiritual significance of the willow, or nature itself, which embodies 'regeneration and faith'.[16] 'Split at the top with two sections that curve toward each other like cupped hands' (in the art historian Susan Kuretsky's description), perhaps in natural prayer, the tree holds within itself the promise of life: new, leafy branches shoot off to the right, and a low branch literally supports Jerome's studies. This new life is artistic as well as spiritual, for if St Jerome, scribbling at his desk, may be seen as a figure of the ageing artist, so too can the willow. From its 'hands' spring two branches of his printmaking art, one rendered in drypoint, the other etched. As importantly, the conflation of decay and vitality, natural substance and spiritual ideas, make the willow a perfect emblem of Rembrandt's belief that 'all living things become richer through the accumulation of age'.[17]

Claude Lorrain was a seventeenth-century landscape painter who would have agreed with Rembrandt's evaluation of the richness of aged nature, though he invested his landscapes with allusions to antique cultures as well. Born in France, he moved as a young man to Italy and remained there for most of his life. He sketched the countryside around Rome and then combined the motifs he had captured into fictive, 'ideal' landscapes more perfect than any found in nature.

Claude Lorrain, *Two Willow Trees on the Bank of a River*, c. 1660–65, pen and brown ink and brown wash over black chalk.

While these works ostensibly depict scenes from classical or biblical mythology, the landscape is the real focus; Claude is art-historically significant for making landscape a legitimate genre of painting in its own right. His oil paintings of classical idylls typically exhibit a standard compositional formula: a coulisse on the left or right side of the fore-ground, often a screen of trees ('coulisse' is a theatre term for a piece of stage scenery jutting out from the wings); a middle ground with some significant feature, whether a building or figural group; a further plane; and, lastly, luminous distance. Using bridges, roads and other devices, these works lead the spectator's eye gradually into the distance, tracing a poetic journey into distant space and time, not unlike Ma Yuan's but more replete with detail and incident. These paintings were immense-ly influential, inspiring the later taste for the picturesque and the English landscape garden. It is his sketches, however, that concern us here.

Claude's drawings (and some paintings) taken directly from nature were important precedents for those later artists, such as Constable and the Impressionists, who were committed to recording light and atmosphere in front of the motif itself. The art historian Kenneth Clark described Claude's sketches as exhibiting 'a visual responsive-ness hardly different from that of the Impressionists',[18] and the artist was known to have spent hours in the landscape watching the chang-ing effects of light on trees. In the 1660s, the decade of his greatest masterpieces, he produced studies after nature of a 'great freedom'[19] – loose, lyrical, intensely responsive and sensuous works. The willowy character of these sketches may be seen in a gorgeous golden-toned drawing of brown ink and wash over black chalk. Two pollarded willows frame a view over a river and into the countryside beyond, in which a small building, a stately tree and some hills are sketched in faintly. The left willow's trunk has split into a precariously leaning, dry-looking husk which is nevertheless sending out new leaves and a more upright, serpentine segment, from the top of which sinuous branches weave into the sky. The trunk and main branch of the right willow, which leans into the scene, flings forth its supple wands, which unfurl out beyond the brown ink in black chalk lines that transform, as our eye follows them, into outlines of clouds and promised foliage. Inviting the eye to explore their forms, Claude's willows fill in the world around them. All the drama framed by the arboreal coulisses in his finished paintings is embodied here in the dancing willows, which work as a frame but insinuate themselves, literally and figuratively, as the objects – or really the lively subjects – of our attention and affection.

Claude was described by John Constable as 'the most perfect land-scape painter the world ever saw',[20] and in the nineteenth-century English painter's work pollard willows also have a privileged place. Constable included willows in his list of beloved sights and sounds: 'the sound of water escaping from Mill dams, etc., Willows, Old rotten banks, slimy posts and brickwork. I love such things.' He declared he would paint them always, for they 'have always been my delight'.[21] Constable's goal was to paint portraits of nature in all its forms and elements. In *A Woman by an Old Willow Tree at Ham, Surrey* of 1834, the artist seems to invoke both Claude's impulse to humanize trees and the long-standing association of willows with female figures to create a half-human portrait of a tree. Drawn in brown ink on off-white paper, the sketch offers a warm, intimate view of an old pollard – cracked, hollowed and worn but still thriving, its foliage swirling in the wind. To the left of the trunk, and visually joined to it, is an old woman. The shape of her cape and skirt echo that of the hollow in the trunk, as though she has just left her arboreal habitation; the cross-hatching of her attire and the tree's interior cements the association, as does the willow basket she carries and what may even be her willow hat. Like a grand-maternal figure, then, the willow becomes the origin and point of return for local rambles. Rooted in and marking a particu-lar place, and hosting a *genius loci*, the pollarded willow is a sign of Constable country.

Constable was not alone in appreciating the picturesque qualities of the willow and its 'marking' function: Camille Corot, the mid-nineteenth-century French landscape painter who drew on the tradition of Claude but paved the way for the Impressionists with his

John Constable, *A Woman by an Old Willow Tree at Ham, Surrey*, 1834, pen and bistre ink on paper.

Camille Corot, *Willows at the Water's Edge*, c. 1855, oil on canvas.

plein-air (outdoor) painting, was a devotee who particularly loved what one British writer described as the 'gauzy veil' willow foliage casts over a landscape, creating 'subtle effects of light'.[22] In *Willows at the Water's Edge*, everything is suffused with a silvery-gold, shimmery ambience. The pollarded willows rise along the shore of the river like the ancestral bones of the spirit of the place, marking the spot and frothing delicate feathery foliage like screens of memory or like the soft, splayed bristles of the painter's brush caressing the canvas with a literally and figuratively 'light touch'. The shadowy glade or passage they fringe, opening just left of centre, draws the eye through the willowy veil into tranquil depths where willow silhouettes read as the pointed arches of a serene, organic Gothic edifice.

Corot was influenced by the advent of photography, and the similarity between his delicately lit and soft-focused canvases and daguerreotypes has been noted. In the early twentieth century, Edward Steichen and other photographers associated with the Pictorialist movement claimed photography's status as a fine art by rejecting the unmanipulated, focused, mechanical look of 'straight' photography and making works that resembled paintings and drawings. The labour-intensive printing processes they favoured allowed them to create soft focus and draw out areas of light and dark while emphasizing the handmade quality of the image. Along with Alfred Stieglitz, Steichen was a leading member of the Photo-Secession group in New York, a contributor to Stieglitz's journal *Camera Work*, and a founder of the Little Galleries of the Photo-Secession. Intriguingly, willow had an emblematic place in the articulation of Photo-Secession principles. The Little Galleries were host to exhibitions of leading European modernists, including Matisse and Picasso, as well as contemporary photography. While the exhibits changed, the galleries had one constant fixture: a bronze bowl full of pussy willows and other branches.[23] Their significance remains obscure, but the brown and grey hues and Aesthetic lineage of these spring branches may have evoked the colour and nineteenth-century inspiration of many Pictorialist prints; they also

Edward Steichen, *Pussy Willow*, 1901, gum platinum or carbon print.

embodied what one *Camera Work* contributor dubbed a 'pussy willow quality of focus',[24] and must have seemed a fitting emblem for a more organic, less mechanical, vision of photography as a medium.

In *Pussy Willow* of 1901, Steichen used willow to suggest the cross-fertilization of mediums that gave rise to the Pictorialist photograph.

Claude Monet, *Weeping Willow, Giverny, c.* 1920, oil on canvas.

In the print, whose rich tones and 'pussy willow' focus have been compared to charcoal drawing[25] (in other words, to tonal drawing with burnt willow wood), the nude figure of a young girl crouches over a vase of pussy willows. Like the budding catkins, her nubile body is in the process of unfurling, not yet fully formed. Emerging from the amorphous ground of the photograph, both plant and girl are brought into being through the action of light – technically, in the development of the photograph, and metaphorically in the implicit photosensitivity of plant and girl. Here the pussy willow's soft brushes embody the

Pictorialist way of seeing and making art, offering a 'photo-synthesis' of drawing, painting and photography in which the carefully orchestrated action of light on sensitive surfaces triggers an aesthetic and erotic awakening.

Constable, Corot, photography, Japanese prints and the aesthetics and poetics associated with these artists and mediums all influenced Claude Monet, who attempted to capture fleeting moments in particular places in paint, and who revelled in the intertwining of water, foliage and sky. Monet spent the last decades of his life in his garden at Giverny painting its weeping-willow-fringed lily pond. A contemporary described the pool as a 'magic hollow' in which the light the artist loved was 'reflected with all its splendours and its mysteries ... surrounded by the foliage of willows'.[26] It is generally agreed that in the *nymphéas* (water lily) paintings, Monet attained 'a depth of meaning' hitherto lacking in his scenes of modern life and leisure.[27] His garden facilitated contemplation and self-reflection, and paintings of the pool's reflections – paintings of nature's paintings – invited meditation on the nature of the work of art itself. Monet's 'endlessly repeated attempt to seize the reflections in his pool' has been likened, by a number of art historians, to the myth of Narcissus, who fell in love with a watery image.[28] In poetry, philosophy and criticism of the time, Narcissus's attempt to grasp the ideal beloved in the still waters of a pool was seen as emblematic of the male artist's attempt to merge with female nature, to bridge the gap between object and image, to attain a state of imaginary plenitude. If the story is equally one of frustration and loss (Narcissus can never capture the image), it never - theless ends with a beautiful metamorphosis.

Bending over his pool to paint, Monet was a Narcissus. Intriguingly, so was the willow. A number of authors of the period (and earlier) regarded the weeping willow as the 'Narcissus of the plants',[29] and the art historian Steven Levine has argued that the ageing Monet identified with the mournful weeping willow, particularly in the late, large-scale paintings he produced for the French state. For if in the late 1890s and early 1900s the garden at Giverny was a place of undisturbed tranquillity, beauty and aesthetic contemplation, its serenity captured in painting after painting of the artist's Japanese bridge and weeping willows reflected in the tranquil waters of the pool, the solace it offered was soon invaded by loss and death. In 1907 Monet started to lose his sight; in 1911 his second wife died; in 1914 his son died unexpectedly; and in the same year the First World War began. Although Monet stayed in Giverny painting, the war was inescapable. Friends and relatives were at the front, and the artist read the newspaper anxiously every day. He could hear the gunfire at Amiens from his garden, and sometimes saw convoys of the wounded on the road he had to cross to reach his pond.[30] He feared for the garden itself; death had invaded paradise.

In the immediate post-war period, Monet painted a series of weeping willow pictures which have been read as works of mourning – not only for the artist's personal losses, but for the brutal and senseless slaughter of a generation of young men. While the weeping willow is a conventional image of grief, Monet anthropomorphizes his trees which embody the suffering of the soldiers and perhaps even excoriate the artist himself for his narcissistic self-absorption in his work. Some of the paintings exhibit scarred and bloody flesh-coloured willow trunks twisting in enveloping, even suffocating, foliage the colour of mustard gas. A less obviously anthropomorphic but equally horrific painting from around 1920, *Weeping Willow, Giverny*, captures the chaos of the front in a hellish scene in which everything is disordered. The pool, the colour of blood, seems more fiery than watery, and dry, red strokes lick like flames up into the foliage which seems to crawl upward in response. The crown of leaves at the top of the image is the heaviest, wettest and most airless part of the painting, inverting our sense of elemental order and gravity, pressing inexorably down and sending the fleeing foliage back into the fray. The weeping willow tresses, painted in 'anguished, writhing strokes',[31] are caught between two hostile forces in an image of almost unbearable pressure.

The great cycle of paintings for the Orangerie, on which he worked from 1914 to 1926 and which were installed only after his death, was Monet's attempt to recuperate all the losses of the last decades of his life, including the at times near total loss of his sight. Conceived of as a kind of 'flowering aquarium',[32] the murals in the two oval rooms envelop the viewer in a watery embrace. The first room is devoted to water lilies; the second, the inner sanctum, to willows. The four paintings – *The Two Willows, Morning with Willows, Clear Morning with Willows* and *Reflections of Trees* – are all 2 m high but of unequal lengths. *Two Willows*, which confronts the entering viewer from the far end of the oval room, is the largest, at 17 m long. On either side the two *Morning with Willows* paintings stretch for 12.75 m; the *Reflections of Trees* is the smallest, at 8.5 m long, and seen last, when one walks into the room and turns around.

Within their broken ellipse, the immersive paintings depict different atmospheric states, times of the day and moods. They also embody the inherent contradictions of Monet's artistic project to 'materialize' light: the heavily worked, dry surfaces of the canvases confront the viewer with a materiality, opacity and density that nevertheless manage to image 'immaterial light', 'transparent water' and 'vibrating air'.[33] The cycle has given rise to conflicting interpretations. The brushstrokes in the Orangerie paintings are less tormented than those of the immediate post-war period, the colours less violent, and some regard these works as achieving a peaceful synthesis of elements (water, air, light, vegetation) and orientations (the horizontal surface of the pool and its vertical depths), the 'leaves of the bending willows' serving to 'link the floating, multicoloured waterlilies with the drifting, inverted clouds'.[34] Seen up close, however, the saturated world of the painting disintegrates into scribbles and crusts, the water's 'translucent depths' disappearing 'into a chaos of desiccated pigment'.[35] At a distance the environing blues are equally disorienting: the horizontal plane (the surface of the pool) has been tilted vertically in the paintings, leaving the viewer unmoored; read another way, the surrounding water threatens to drown the viewer in the 'aquarium'.

The struggle the paintings embody is most tangible in *The Two Willows* and *Reflections of Trees*, which represent extremes in the cycle

of light depicted. The enormous *Two Willows* is an overpoweringly luminous, 'unearthly' blue; the art historian Virginia Spate describes it as having a 'visionary intensity'.[36] In it the tortured willow trees of the war no longer take centre stage, though they still frame the calmer vision Monet paints. The palette of *Reflections of Trees* is much darker, filled with gloomy blues and violets. Opposite the radiant expanse of *The Two Willows*, the smaller *Reflections of Trees* is murky, material, even morbid. It is a painting of literal and figurative darkness, based on a painting called *Reflections of Willows* painted the year that Monet's son was at Verdun and recalling Monet's deathbed painting of his first wife. Almost literalizing the French term for still water (*les eaux mortes,*

Claude Monet, *Waterlilies* paintings, c. 1914–26, oil on canvas. Top to bottom: *The Two Willows, Morning with Willows, Clear Morning with Willows, Reflections of Trees.*

dead waters), *Reflections of Trees* gives us a Bachelardian image of water 'holding the dead in its substance'.[37] Monet's desire to create a world free of horror, loss and death proves impossible to fulfil; the war may have ended, but its effects lingered.

These monumental works are shaped as much by Monet's medi-tation on sight itself as by their historical context. Spate describes the dainty, rather decorative trees in *The Two Willows* as 'little more than images on the edge of sight or memory'.[38] A contemporary of

Monet's similarly described their foliage as 'eyelashes' framing the vision of the water and shading the upper part of the picture,[39] and we may read them as Monet's acknowledgment of the limits and frailty of the human eye and embodied vision. The fragility of the artist's own sight was a constant problem while he was painting the cycle. Spectacles and operations could not fix his cataracts, and he was terrified by the prospect of total blindness. The 'perfect circle of light' he dreamt of was impossible.[40] In *Reflections of Trees* light is almost entirely extinguished; the only glimmers that remain are the uncannily bright reds of the lilies right of centre, burning in the dark like the eyes of unseen creatures, and the eerie, almost bioluminescent purple-white reflections, like will-o'-the-wisps, haunting the pool. Levine reads the willows in these paintings as figures for the 'body of the aged artist' and as an 'allegory of the mortal struggle to seize the impossible image of his dream'. The ghostly shadow of a willow trunk at the centre figuratively envisions the artist's fading eyesight and mortal frailty in this watery realm that is as much tomb as womb.[41]

Memory links historical, individual and human experience here. In the Orangerie cycle, seeing one painting means turning one's back on another. While this arrangement stresses the physical limits of sight, it also casts memory as a bridge between what lies ahead and behind, spatially and temporally. The willow room's arrangement 'insists', as Spate has shown, 'on the interpenetration of every phase of light in one's consciousness: darkness is thus latent in one's experience of the measureless light of *The Two Willows*, and light is like a memory in the darkness of the *Reflections of Trees*'.[42] Memory allowed Monet both to paint the great panels (he relied on it increasingly as his eyesight failed) and also to become more like the willow, bending over the pool not to see but to weep. And to learn the last lesson on vision in his visionary life: in Andrew Marvell's words, how 'eyes and tears be the same things . . . each the other's difference bears, / These weeping eyes, those seeing tears'.[43]

Conclusion: Willow in the World Garden

As we wind our willowy journey to a close, let us consider a few paradigmatic instances of willow in the gardens of the world where, serving practical or ornamental ends or both, it may act as an imaginary catalyst, evoking reveries or reminiscences of other times, places and states of mind. The species, garden types and garden architectures we will explore in these last pages suggest both the history and, today more than ever, the necessity of imagining other worlds and other ways of engaging with the world through gardens.

Salix babylonica, the classic Chinese weeping willow, now a staple of botanical gardens and found in pure or hybrid form throughout the Western world, has long been an essential feature of Eastern gardens, where its graceful foliage often overhangs still or moving waters. Native to China, the tree travelled along the Silk Road to the West, in a slow arboreal migration occasionally hastened by a traveller carrying seeds or twigs. The poet Alexander Pope supposedly introduced it to England in the 1720s: he had received a basket of fruit from Smyrna from a friend and, seeing that one of the wands was alive, he planted it in the grounds of his villa in Twickenham. There it throve and grew into a world-renowned specimen that framed the entrance to his equally famous, lavishly decorated grotto. Cuttings from this willow made their way to gardens throughout England and beyond; as one visitor in 1789 wrote, 'a thousand slips are annually transmitted to the most distant quarters of the globe, and during the present year the Empress of Russia has planted some in her own garden at St Petersburgh'.[1]

The Governor of St Helena took cuttings from trees propagated from Pope's and planted them on the island, where they became Napoleon's 'favorite shady arbor during his imprisonment' and there-after, for a brief time, his gravesite (his remains were later returned to France). According to legend, one of them was uprooted during a violent storm the night the conqueror of Europe died.[2] These willows, so vividly imbued with history, in turn became 'the most souvenir-hunted plants in the nineteenth century',[3] providing cuttings or simply remembrance, and their clones too becoming cherished specimens. An album of pressed flowers and leaves collected by a traveller in 1846, for example, contains a dried spray of leaves 'from the tree which waved over the grave of Napoleon's Tomb at St Helena, and now transplanted to a small garden at the Hospital des Invalides'.

When Pope's villa was destroyed in 1808, his willow had nearly reached the end of its life. The English Romantic painter J.M.W. Turner described taking a slip from the ageing tree:

Now to destruction doom'd thy peaceful grott
Pope's willow bending to the earth forgot

Dried *Salix babylonica* leaves in album of pressed flowers assembled by S. I. Crafton.

opposite: Salix babylonica in the Orto Botanico di Padova, Italy.

Save one weak scion by my fostering care
Nursed into life.[4]

Turner built his own villa in Twickenham and planted it with willows, while the dead stump of Pope's tree was placed inside his 'peaceful grott', where it still remains in state. Although it is now thought that the first weeping willow was brought to Britain around 1701 by a surgeon with the East India Company, and that Pope's willow was a gift from the author's landlord rather than a sprout delivered literally in a basket,[5] Pope's tree nevertheless has an important place in garden history and was a progenitor of plants throughout Europe and America.

The story of Pope's willow and its proliferating cuttings is truly a willowy one, spanning centuries and the northern hemisphere, and

Matteo Ripa, print from *Thirty-Six Views of the Imperial Palace at Jehol*, 1711–13, engraving on thin China paper.

encompassing poets' retreats, artists' gardens, states of exile and graves. Along with the tree came a new style of garden: the English landscape garden or the *jardin anglo-chinois*, as it was known in France. Early eighteenth-century engravings of the Chinese emperor's summer retreat at Jehol (now known as Chengde) introduced Europeans to a style of landscape design radically different from their preferred formal, symmetrical layouts. The carefully crafted 'seeming naturalness and rusticity'[6] of the irregular imperial gardens, in which the 'imperial' willow played a key role, inspired a desire for such pleasing views at home. English gardeners created landscapes based on Claude's paintings and what they learned from the Chinese, constructing terrains and framed views that inspired reverie. Weeping willows became a familiar site in these 'dressed gardens and pleasure-grounds' of the eighteenth and nineteenth centuries.[7] William Gilpin advised gardeners to use them to adorn 'some romantic footpath bridge, which it half conceals, or some glassy pool, over which it hangs its streaming foliage'.[8]

Weeping willows and the *jardin anglo-chinois* are paradigmatic instances of the willow's ability not only to bridge and hybridize the traditions and poetics of East and West but also, by offering an aesthetic alternative, to introduce, for some, at least, a new way of seeing and relating to both local and global landscapes. Another sort of willowy garden that has fascinated the West for centuries and awakened wonder, if not as much emulation as the Chinese garden, is the Mesoamerican chinampa, an indigenous form of landscape engineering that combines agriculture and the powerful dream-image of the 'floating garden'.

Considered marvels by Spanish colonizers, chinampas, or 'floating gardens', were cultivated by the Aztecs in the southern Basin of Mexico. Jesuit missionaries described chinampas as buoyant platforms, their bases woven out of reeds and then loaded with soil to create mobile, continually irrigated fields. When he visited Mexico in 1803, the naturalist Alexander von Humboldt noted that such floating gardens, built on 'rafts formed of reeds' and 'driven about by the winds', were disappearing in favour of alternatives fixed at the margins of lakes and extending to great sizes (100 m x 5–6 m), but that Mexico City was 'richly supplied with eatables' from both.[9] By the end of the nineteenth century most commentators described anchored rather than itinerant chinampas which, they theorized, may have become fixed in place through the growth of the roots of the willow trees planted around their perimeters for stability. Moored or wandering, the idea of lush, floating, willow-fringed gardens – perhaps, according to Humboldt, the invention of a people who wished to escape their

The Tolteca at Cholula, *Historia Tolteca-Chichimeca*, 1547–60, pigment on European paper.

Canals with chinampas in San Luis Tlaxialtemalco, Mexico.

enemies by living on a lake – evoke serene images of peaceful plenitude as well as admiration for Aztec ingenuity.

The associations of the willowy chinampas with protection, inventiveness and sustainable havens is indebted to Aztec lore, in which the Mexica once pacified a powerful neighbouring people by constructing a splendid floating garden, and in which various 'promised land' sites including Tenochtitlan (where Mexico City is today) were marked, among other signs, by the presence of 'white willow' (*huexotl*), often surrounding a spring. In indigenous manuscripts, such places are frequently indicated with glyphs that include a willow. A manuscript created two to four decades after the Spanish conquest of the Aztecs in 1521 recounts the migration of the Tolteca-Chichimeca from Tollan to Cholula in 1168 and represents the chosen city by a hill glyph, painted in luscious blues and greens and dotted with flowers, framed by white reeds on the left and a white willow on the right, its name written in Nahuatl in the scroll above ('Iztac Uexotr' or Iztac Huexotl).[10]

Possibly cultivated as early as 100 BCE, chinampa agriculture reached its height in the fifteenth century, though it still survives in places, most famously in Xochimilco, the Mexican 'Venice'. The fields

that the willows fringe are planted with a variety of crops and are almost continually productive, farmers swapping in young plants from seedbeds as soon as others are harvested. While not categor - ically ruling out the historical existence of actual floating gardens, the geographer Philip Crossley has studied the history and botany

Canals and chinampas in Xochimilco, Mexico.

of chinampas and contends that most of them were probably a form of wetland or shallow lake agriculture in which earth plots with reinforced edges were separated by canals, as they are today. The distinctive willows (*Salix bonplandiana*, ahuexotl) that are planted at the corners and along the perimeter of each garden, rather than anchoring the chinampas, serve to stabilize their banks and play an increasingly important role today as water levels decrease.[11]

Throughout this book we have seen the willow's key role in agriculture – as support for vines and other plants, material for implements (mostly baskets), animal fodder and fuel – as well as in myth and aesthetics. In the case of the chinampas, the willows both support the fields and help create their evocative image of floating paradises rooted in Aztec legend and so fascinating to European colonists, their willow borders, as we have seen in other contexts, screening them off from the encroaching outer world and delimiting the zone of an alternative consciousness. Yet though marvellous, the 'islands' also seem, today, somewhat funereal. In the distant past, chinampas supplied a large proportion of the maize, vegetables, fruits and flowers necessary to support the urban population, but since the 1950s there has been a drastic reduction in the area devoted to this form of agriculture, the effect of rapid urbanization and economic changes. While still productive, the chinampas in Xochimilco are arguably more important for tourism than farming, as the picturesque traces of a vanished world.

Resistance to environmental and aesthetic degradation has inspired a wave of willow gardening on a small scale, though, in addition to the larger biofiltration and soil remediation projects mentioned in the Introduction. Various species of willow are now a fixture in household and community gardens – literally, in the form of living willow fences, chairs, labyrinths, arbours, domes and other structures which anyone can plant and shape.[12] Such leafy seats and bowers can invoke poetic reveries; in the garden of the childhood home of Shakespeare's wife Anne Hathaway, one can even sit and listen to recordings of the sonnets in the simple dome of a living willow arbour. Others invite activity and creativity; the sculpted, trellised walls of the crown-like willow arbour at Whichford Pottery in Warwickshire incite play and, when periodically trimmed, provide cuttings for other willow projects.

The Auerworldpalast, a living willow structure just outside Auerstedt, Germany, is a communal version of such semi-private bowers. Resembling a Gothic rose window in plan, the 'palace' gently rises in

Willow arbour, Anne Hathaway's Cottage, Shottery, Warwickshire.

Willow arbour by Windrush Willow at Whichford Pottery, Warwickshire.

ascending shaggy arches to create a low, openwork dome. The interior, all cool green light and branching tracery, is filled with rustic seats at the base of the willow columns, on which listeners can sit during the concerts that take place there as well as the full moon celebrations. A collaboration between the artists' collective Sanfte Strukturen and 300 volunteers from around the globe, the Auerworldpalast was built in the spring of 1998 and is still thriving – a monument, as its bilingual, hybrid name suggests, to 'our world' and the potential we have, and

Auerworldpalast, 1998, willow, Auerstedt, Germany.

Auerworldpalast, 1998, willow, Auerstedt, Germany.

which willow helps us recognize, to shape it in collaboration rather than competition with other species.[13]

The *jardin anglo-chinois*, a garden through which to view the world; the chinampa, a garden that *is* a world; and willow structures, living architectures that embody the dream of returning the world, if not to a garden state, then at least to an environmentally sustainable one, all offer perspectives onto poetic and practical possibilities in the world garden. To conclude this leafy tome I cannot, as I would wish, offer you a willow branch in parting. I will, however, urge you to live with and love willow. Buy a willow basket from a local maker or make something from willow wands yourself. Write a letter with a pussy willow pen or plant willow in your garden. Read 'the character for heart'[14] that the willow inscribes on the world, and remember to remember what we as a species have lived through and lost. Above all, be *willowy*: hybridize, enrich and protect our world.

Timeline

145–65 million years ago (Cretaceous period)	Angiosperms appear; dwarf willows make up a significant portion of the flowering plant population
110,000–10,000 years ago (last glacial period)	Glaciers connecting the northern continents melt, spreading willow across the Northern hemisphere
9th or 8th millennium BCE	Willow bast is used to make fishing nets in northern Europe
4500–2000 BCE	Arrowheads in the shape of willow leaves are placed in Stone Age burials
3050–332 BCE	The ancient Egyptians hold an annual raising of the willow festival; various Egyptian medical treatises recommend using willow as an anti-inflammatory
8th century BCE	Homer describes willows as 'fruit-losing' in *The Odyssey*, giving rise to the belief that willow is a contraceptive, which holds until the later Middle Ages
5th century BCE	Herodotus describes Babylonian coracles made of willow frames covered with skins. Hippocrates recommends chewing willow leaves to relieve the pain of childbirth as well as to reduce post-partum fever, and *Salix alba* is used to treat pain and fever in China
2nd century BCE	Cato the Elder describes the osier field or willow plantation (*salictum*) as one of the most valuable parts of a farm

1st century BCE	Dioscorides describes willow's medicinal properties. In the 50s Julius Caesar writes his *Commentaries on the Gallic War*, containing his account of druidic human sacrifice in giant willow constructions
1st century CE	Pliny the Elder describes the cultivation and uses of willow, including basketry and woven furniture
2nd century	The Chinese pharmacopoeia recommends willow for arthritis and other ailments
7th–early 9th centuries (Tang period in China)	Willow becomes a central figure in Chinese poetry, especially as metaphor for female beauty
9th–11th centuries	Arabic medical treatises include willow-based abortifacients and contraceptives
Late 12th–early 13th centuries	Ma Yuan paints willows
14th century	Pietro Crescenzi describes the usefulness of willows. Japanese medical treatises recommend willow in the treatment of battle wounds
14th–16th centuries	Basketmakers' guilds are formed in many European cities
16th and early 17th centuries	Shakespeare's plays with significant willow scenes and songs, Li Shizhen's *Ben Cao Gang Mu* and John Gerard's *Herbal* are published. The tradition of parading willow *Reuze* (giant effigies) through Flemish towns begins
17th century	The Manchus conquer China and erect the willow palisade, a botanical wall over 1,000 km long. In his print *St Jerome Beside a Pollard Willow*, Rembrandt gives pictorial precedence to the willow tree rather than the saint. Nicholas Culpeper's *Complete Herbal* and John Evelyn's *Sylva* discuss the medical and agricultural uses of willow. Aylett Sammes illustrates the 'Wicker Image' of Caesar's Druids
18th century	The Revd Edward Stone presents a paper on the medicinal applications of *Salix alba* bark to the Royal Society of London. Willow pattern dishes are first

produced by Spode in England, and the willow and urn motif starts to appear on gravestones in New England. Sir James Hall presents a paper tracing the forms of Gothic architecture to rustic willow churches. Alexander Pope plants a weeping willow (*Salix babylonica*), cuttings from which spread the species across Europe and North America

17th–19th centuries (Edo period in Japan)	The willow becomes an important figure in Japanese poetry and the *Ukiyo-e* ('floating world') prints by Hiroshige and others
1800–1850	Johann Andreas Buchner extracts salicin from *Salix*. *Salictum Woburnense*, a catalogue of the Duke of Bedford's *salictum*, or willow arboretum, at Woburn Abbey is published. Boilers for willow are introduced in Britain and America, making the peeling of willow wands easier and faster
1850–1900	William Morris produces willow-themed wallpapers and furnishing fabrics. Dante Gabriel and Christina Rossetti write willow poetry. Otto Lilienthal makes a variety of gliders out of willow and canvas, achieving gliding flight in the 1890s. Louisa Keyser starts selling her baskets through Cohn Emporium in Carson City, Nevada
1900–1925	Charles Rennie and Margaret Macdonald Mackintosh's Willow Tea Rooms open, and Gustav Stickley introduces willow furniture into his Craftsman series. Algernon Blackwood's 'The Willows', Kenneth Grahame's *The Wind in the Willows*, Princesse Marthe Bibesco's *Isvor: The Country of Willows* and Velimir Khlebnikov's 'The Willow Twig' are published. Most of the Somerset willow crop goes to the war effort, and Claude Monet's late willow paintings reflect on the First World War
1925–1950	Stripping machines are introduced for willow. In the Second World War, most of Britain's willow crop goes to support the war effort. W. H. Auden's 'Underneath an Abject Willow' is set to music by Benjamin Britten

1945–today   J.R.R. Tolkien's *Lord of the Rings*, Hubert Selby Jr's *The Willow Tree* and the Harry Potter series (featuring the whomping willow) are published, and the cult classic film *The Wicker Man*, directed by Robin Hardy, is released. Environmental artists including Patrick Dougherty start to work with willow structures, and contemporary basketmakers explore willow's possibilities. Willow is increasingly used for biofiltration, bioengineering and biofuel

References

Introduction: Natural History

1 Christopher Newsholme, *Willows: The Genus Salix* (London, 1992), pp. 10–12.
2 Archie Miles, *Silva: The Tree in Britain* (London, 1999), p. 188.
3 J. L. Knapp, *The Journal of a Naturalist*, 2nd edn (London, 1829), p. 397.
4 Miles, *Silva*, p. 58.
5 John Evelyn, *Sylva; or, A Discourse of Forest-Trees* (London, 1670), p. 88.
6 Carl von Linné, *Species Plantarum*, 2nd edn (Stockholm, 1763), vol. II, p. 1449.
7 William Jackson Hooker, *The British Flora; Comprising the Phaenogamous, or Flowering Plants, and the Ferns*, 2nd edn (London, 1831), p. 409.
8 Newsholme, *Willows*, p. 23.
9 Marcus Porcius Cato, *On Agriculture*, trans. William David Hooper (Cambridge, MA, 1934), p. 7 (book I, section 1.7).
10 Pliny the Elder, *Natural History*, trans. H. Rackham (London, 1945), vol. IV, p. 499 (book 16, chapter 67).
11 John Gerard, *The Herbal; or, Generall historie of plantes* (London, 1597), pp. 1202–04.
12 Pliny the Elder, *Natural History*, trans. W.H.S. Jones (London, 1956), vol. VII, p. 45 (book 24, chapter 37).
13 Evelyn, *Sylva*, pp. 86, 88, 90, 86.
14 Hooker, *British Flora*, p. 409.
15 James Forbes, *Salictum Woburnense; or, A Catalogue of Willows, Indigenous and Foreign, in the Collection of the Duke of Bedford, Woburn Abbey* (London, 1829), p. 49.
16 William Scaling, *The Salix or Willow in a Series of Papers: Part 1* (London, 1871), pp. 4–5 of the 'Descriptive Catalogue'.
17 William Culpeper, *Culpeper's English Physician; and Complete Herbal* (London, 1789), p. 386.
18 Evelyn, *Sylva*, p. 89.
19 Henry David Thoreau, *Faith in a Seed: The Dispersion of Seeds and Other Late Natural History Writings*, ed. Bradley P. Dean (Washington, DC, 1993), pp. 56–7.

20 Miles, *Silva*, p. 330.

21 J. C. Loudon, *Arboretum et Fruticetum Britannicum; or, The Trees and Shrubs of Britain*, 2nd edn (London, 1854), vol. III, p. 1462.

22 Fred Hageneder, *The Spirit of Trees: Science, Symbiosis and Inspiration* (Edinburgh, 2000), p. 125.

23 Isidore of Seville, *The Etymologies of Isidore of Seville*, trans. Stephen A. Barney et al. (Cambridge, 2006), p. 346 (XVII.vii.47–8).

24 Thoreau, *Faith in a Seed*, p. 61.

25 Wilhelm Mannhardt, *Der Baumkultus der Germanen und ihrer Nachbartstämme* (Berlin, 1875), p. 32.

26 Sir James Frazer, *The Golden Bough: A Study in Magic and Religion*, abbreviated edn (New York, 1996), pp. 791, 632.

27 Edmund Stone, 'An Account of the Success of the Bark of the Willow in the Cure of Agues', *Philosophical Transactions of the Royal Society of London*, 53 (1763), pp. 195–200, p. 198.

28 K. C. Nicolaou and T. Montagnon, *Molecules that Changed the World* (Weinheim, 2008), pp. 23–4.

29 Dioscorides Pedanius, *The Greek Herbal of Dioscorides*, trans. John Goodyer, ed. Robert T. Gunther (New York, 1959), p. 75.

30 Pliny, *Natural History*, vol. VII, p. 45 (book 24, chapter 37).

31 William Turner, *The second parte of William Turners herball* (Cologne, 1562), p. 126.

32 Culpeper, *Culpeper's English Physician*, p. 386.

33 Miles, *Silva*, p. 266.

34 Dioscorides, *Greek Herbal*, p. 75; Pliny, *Natural History*, vol. VII, p. 47 (book 24, chapter 37).

35 Homer, *The Odyssey*, trans. A. T. Murray (Cambridge, MA, 1945), vol. II, p. 381 (book 10, line 510); Hugo Rahner, *Greek Myths and Christian Mystery* (London, 1963), pp. 286–98.

36 Pliny, *Natural History*, vol. IV, p. 461 (book 16, chapter 46).

37 John M. Riddle, *Contraception and Abortion from the Ancient World to the Renaissance* (Cambridge, MA, 1994), pp. 85, 89, 97, 127, 129.

38 Jennifer Wurges and Rebecca J. Frey, 'White Willow', in *The Gale Encyclopedia of Alternative Medicine*, 3rd edn (Detroit, MI, 2009), vol. IV, pp. 2375–7, p. 2375.

39 *Chinese–English Chinese Traditional Medical World–Ocean Dictionary* (Taiyuan, 1995), p. 1171.

40 Li Shizhen, *Compendium of Materia Medica (Bencao Gangmu)*, trans. Luo Xiwen (Beijing, 2003), vol. V, pp. 3084–5, 3089.

41 Case 41, Edward Smith Surgical Papyrus, New York Academy of Medicine, trans. James P. Allen, available at http://archive.nlm.nih.gov.

42 Andrew Edmund Goble, 'War and Injury: The Emergence of Wound Medicine in Medieval Japan', *Monumenta Nipponica*, LX/3 (2005), pp. 297–338, p. 315.

43 Aulus Cornelius Celsus, *De Medicina*, trans. W. G. Spencer (London, 1961), vol. II, p. 287 (book 6, chapter 18, section 9 C10)

44 Ms III.33 (C64) (*Yangsheng fang*), in *Early Chinese Medical Literature: The Mawangdui Medical Manuscripts*, trans. Donald J. Harper (London, 1998), p. 339.

45 See Worldwatch Institute, 'Residents of Inner Mongolia Find New Hope in the Desert', 14 August 2007, www.worldwatch.org; Joy Abrahams, 'WET Systems for Waste Purification and Resource Production', 1 October 1996, www.permaculture.co.uk; and various articles in the United Nations' forestry journal's special issue on poplars and willows, *Unasylva*, 221 (2005), www.fao.org/docrep.

46 S. J. Hanley, 'Willow', in *Energy Crops*, ed. Nigel G. Halford and Angela Karp (Cambridge, 2011), pp. 259–74, pp. 270–71.

1 Rites of Spring and Mourning

1 Richard H. Wilkinson, *Symbol and Magic in Egyptian Art* (London, 1994), pp. 90–91.

2 Ludwig Keimer, 'L'arbre tjeret: est il réellement le saule égyptien (*Salix safsaf* Forsk.)?', *Bulletin de l'Institut français d'archéologie orientale*, 31 (1931), pp. 177–237, pp. 211, 197.

3 Charles M. Skinner, *Myths and Legends of Flowers, Trees, Fruits, and Plants in All Ages and All Climes* (Philadelphia, PA, 1925), p. 296.

4 Alexander Porteous, *Forest Folklore, Mythology, and Romance* (New York, 1928), p. 64.

5 Skinner, *Myths*, p. 296.

6 Hugo Rahner, *Greek Myths and Christian Mystery* (London, 1963), pp. 291–2.

7 Bruce M. Metzger and Roland E. Murphy, eds, *The New Oxford Annotated Bible with the Apocryphal / Deuterocanonical Books: New Revised Standard Edition* (New York, 1991), p. 792, lines 1–2.

8 Hui-Lin Li, *Shade and Ornamental Trees: Their Origin and History* (Philadelphia, PA, 1996), p. 45.

9 Lucy Hooper, ed., *The Lady's Book of Flowers and Poetry* (New York, 1842), p. 239.

10 Rahner, *Greek Myths*, p. 314.

11 Angelo de Gubernatis, *La Mythologie des plantes; ou, Les Légendes du règne végétal* (Paris, 1882), vol. II, p. 5.

12 Wilhelm Mannhardt, *Der Baumkultus der Germanen und ihrer Nachbartstämme* (Berlin, 1875), p. 293. Mannhardt's treatment of pussy willows in European ritual is extensive; see pp. 257–93.

13 Ibid., p. 257.

14 Sir James Frazer, *The Golden Bough: A Study in Magic and Religion*, abbreviated edn (New York, 1996), pp. 146–7.

15 Mannhardt, *Baumkultus*, pp. 193, 199, 207.

16 Frazer, *Golden Bough*, pp. 148–9.

17 Joseph Strutt, *The Sports and Pastimes of the People of England* (London, 1801), p. 282.

18 Princess Marthe Bibesco, *Isvor, The Country of Willows*, trans. Hamish Miles (London, 1924), pp. 105–06, 121.

19 Mannhardt, *Baumkultus*, pp. 251–2.

20 Patricia Bjaaland Welch, *Chinese Art: A Guide to Motifs and Visual Imagery* (Tokyo, 2008), p. 41.

21 John C. Huntington, *The Circle of Bliss: Buddhist Meditational Art* (Chicago, 2003), p. 344.

22 John Batchelor, 'Items of Ainu Folk-Lore', *Journal of American Folk-Lore*, VII/24 (1894), pp. 15–44, p. 25.

23 J. Batchelor, 'Specimens of Ainu Folk-lore', *Transactions of the Asiatic Society of Japan*, 16 (1889), pp. 111–59, p. 116.

24 Teiichi Yagashita, *Yanagi no bunkashi* (Kyoto, 1995), pp. 35, 60, 112–16, 56–7.

25 Herodotus, *The Histories*, trans. Aubrey de Sélincourt, rev. John Marincola (Harmondsworth, 1996), p. 236 (book 4, section 67).

26 Brian Baumann, *Divine Knowledge: Buddhist Mathematics According to the Anonymous Manual of Mongolian Astrology and Divination* (Leiden, 2008), p. 280.

27 *Wandering Spirits: Chen Shiyuan's Encyclopedia of Dreams*, trans. Richard E. Strassberg (Berkeley, CA, 2008), p. 58.

28 Frances Densmore, *Chippewa Customs* (Minneapolis, MN, 1970), p. 52.

29 Fang Jing Pei, *Symbols and Rebuses in Chinese Art: Figures, Bugs, Beasts, and Flowers* (Berkeley, CA, 2004), p. 191; Wolfram Eberhard, *A Dictionary of Chinese Symbols: Hidden Symbols in Chinese Life and Thought*, trans. G. L. Campbell (London, 1986), p. 314.

30 Keimer, 'L'arbre tjeret', pp. 200–04.

31 Melvin R. Gilmore, 'Uses of Plants by the Indians of the Missouri River Region', in *Thirty-Third Annual Report of the Bureau of American Ethnology to the Secretary of the Smithsonian Institution* (Washington, DC, 1919), pp. 43–154, pp. 73–4.

32 Edwin Dethlefsen and James Deetz, 'Death's Heads, Cherubs, and Willow Trees: Experimental Archaeology in Colonial Cemeteries', *American Antiquity*, XXXI/4 (1966), pp. 502–10, pp. 503, 508.

33 Welch, *Chinese Art*, p. 41.

34 Skinner, *Myths*, p. 296.

35 Mannhardt, *Baumkultus*, pp. 42, 26.

36 Johann Georg Krünitz, 'Kirch-Hof', in *Oeconomisch-technologische Encyclopädie, oder Allgemeines System der Stats-, Stadt-, Haus-, und Land-Wirthschaft, und der Kunst-Geschichte* (Berlin, 1786), p. 423, translated by Nina Amstutz.

37 *OED* s.v. 'wicked', adj. 1, 'wick', adj. 1, 'witch', n. 2, 'wicker', n.

38 Skinner, *Myths*, p. 296.

39 Jes Battis, '"She's Not All Grown Yet": Willow as Hybrid/Hero in *Buffy the Vampire Slayer*', *Slayage*, 11/4 [8] (2003), http://slayageonline.com, accessed 17 March 2012.

40 Yagashita, *Yanagi*, p. 171.

41 Mannhardt, *Baumkultus*, pp. 69, 104; see also W.R.S. Ralston, 'Forest and Field Myths', *Contemporary Review*, 31 (1877–8), pp. 520–37, p. 525.

42 Patricia Monaghan, *Encyclopedia of Goddesses and Heroines* (Santa Barbara, CA, 2010), vol. II, p. 559.

43 Percy Manning, 'Some Oxfordshire Seasonal Festivals: With Notes on Morris-Dancing in Oxfordshire', *Folklore*, VIII/4 (1897), pp. 307–24, p. 311.

44 Mannhardt, *Baumkultus*, pp. 323, 343; Frazer, *Golden Bough*, p. 149.

45 Henry Balfour, 'A Primitive Musical Instrument', *The Reliquary and Illustrated Archaeologist* (1896), pp. 221–4, p. 221.

46 Mannhardt, *Baumkultus*, pp. 342–3, 345.

47 Ola Kai Ledang, 'Revival and Innovation: The Case of the Norwegian Seljefløyte', *Yearbook for Traditional Music*, 18 (1986), pp. 145–56.

48 Simon Chadwick, 'The Early Irish Harp', *Early Music*, XXXVI/4 (2008), pp. 521–31.

49 Victor King Chestnut, 'Plants Used by the Indians of Mendocino County, California', *Contributions from the U.S. National Herbarium*, VII/3 (1902), pp. 295–408, p. 332.

50 Fred Hageneder, *The Spirit of Trees: Science, Symbiosis and Inspiration* (Edinburgh, 2000), p. 128.

51 James Legge, trans. and ed., *The She King*, vol. IV of *The Chinese Classics with a Translation, Critical and Exegetical Notes, Prolegomena, and Copious Indexes*, 2nd edn (Taipei, 1971), p. 407.

52 Jerome Silbergeld, 'Kung Hsien's Self-Portrait in Willows, with Notes on the Willow in Chinese Painting and Literature', *Artibus Asiae*, XLII/1 (1980), pp. 5–38, p. 12.

53 Richard L. Edmonds, 'The Willow Palisade', *Annals of the Association of American Geographers*, LXIX/4 (1979), pp. 569–621. See also David Sneath, 'Beyond the Willow Palisade: Manchuria and the History of China's Inner Asian Frontier', *Asian Affairs*, XXXIV/1 (2003), pp. 3–11.

54 Silbergeld, 'Kung Hsien's Self-Portrait', p. 29.

55 David Quintner, *Willow! Solving the Mystery of Our 200-Year Love Affair with the Willow Pattern* (Burnstown, ON, 1997), p. 34.

56 *French Caricature and the French Revolution, 1789–1799*, exh. cat., Grunwald Center for the Graphic Arts, Los Angeles (1988), pp. 197–8.

57 For more detail, see the Burke and Fox entries in Roland G. Thorne, *The House of Commons 1790–1820*, 5 vols (London, 1986).

58 Archie Miles, *Sylva: The Tree in Britain* (London, 1999), p. 291.

59 Simon Schama, *Landscape and Memory* (London, 1995), p. 573.

60 Frank Coffee, *Forty Years on the Pacific* (New York, 1920), p. 185.

61 'Partition of the Western Pacific', *Edinburgh Review*, CXCI/392 (1900), pp. 478–509, p. 500.

62 Hugh Hastings Romilly, *The Western Pacific and New Guinea: Notes on the Natives, Christian and Cannibal, with Some Account of the Old Labour Trade*, 2nd edn (London, 1887), pp. 141–2.

63 Keith A. P. Sandiford, 'Introduction', in *The Imperial Game: Cricket, Culture and Society*, ed. Brian Stoddart and Keith A. P. Sandiford, pp. 1–8 (Manchester, 1998), p. 1.

64 Richard Cashman, 'The Subcontinent', in *The Imperial Game*, pp. 116–33, p. 123.

65 Guy Hardy Scholefield, *The Pacific, its Past and Future, and the Policy of the Great Powers from the Eighteenth Century* (London, 1919), p. 199.
66 Julius Caesar, *Caesar's Commentaries on the Gallic War*, trans. T. Rice Holmes (London, 1908), p. 183.
67 See Ronald Hutton, *Blood and Mistletoe: The History of the Druids in Britain* (New Haven, CT, 2009), pp. 3–5.
68 Aylett Sammes, *Britannia Antiqua Illustrata; or, The Antiquities of Ancient Britain* (London, 1676), pp. 104–6, emphasis in original.
69 Hutton, *Blood and Mistletoe*, p. 70.
70 Robert Southey, *The Book of the Church*, 2nd edn (London, 1824), vol. 1, pp. 8–9.
71 'Superstitions of the Druids', *Saturday Magazine*, 1/10 (1832), pp. 73–4.
72 'Ancienne Religion des Gaulois', *Magasin pittoresque*, 1/13 (1833), pp. 97–8.
73 For a few examples, see Jonathan Brooke, 'Providentialist Nationalism and Juvenile Mission Literature, 1840–1870', available at http://henry martyn.dns-systems.net, accessed 13 August 2013.
74 Mannhardt, *Baumkultus*, p. 514.
75 Robert Graves, *The White Goddess: A Historical Grammar of Poetic Myth*, ed. Grevel Lindop (London, 1997), p. 53.
76 Ernst Benkard, *Undying Faces: A Collection of Death Masks*, trans. Margaret M. Green (London, 1929), pp. 18–27, quotation on p. 27.
77 Jennifer Woodward, 'Funeral Rituals in the French Renaissance', *Renaissance Studies*, IX/4 (1995), pp. 385–94, p. 387.
78 'Art-Rambles in Belgium, Chapter 3', *Art Journal*, 45 (1865), pp. 277–80, p. 277.
79 Mannhardt, *Baumkultus*, p. 523.
80 Nicole Parrot, *Mannequins*, trans. Sheila de Vallée (London, 1982), p. 35.
81 Anatole France, *Le Mannequin d'osier* (Paris, 1898), pp. 125, 163, 167.

2 Willowy Forms

1 Lise Bender Jørgensen, 'Europe', in *The Cambridge History of Western Textiles*, ed. David Jenkins (Cambridge, 2003), vol. 1, p. 54.
2 J. Ernest Phythian, *Trees in Nature, Myth and Art* (London, 1907), p. 92.
3 Princess Marthe Bibesco, *Isvor: The Country of Willows*, trans. Hamish Miles (London, 1924), p. 145.
4 Ralph Shanks, *Indian Baskets of Central California: Art, Culture, and History*, ed. Lisa Woo Shanks (Novato, CA, 2006), p. 10.
5 Catherine S. Fowler, 'Foreword', in Mary Lee Fulkerson, *Weavers of Tradition and Beauty: Basketmakers of the Great Basin* (Reno, NV, 1995), pp. ix–x.
6 Shanks, *Indian Baskets*, p. 25.
7 Victor King Chestnut, 'Plants Used by the Indians of Mendocino County, California', *Contributions from the U.S. National Herbarium*, VII/3 (1902), p. 331.

8 Evan M. Maurer, 'Determining Quality in Native American Art', in *The Arts of the North American Indian: Native Traditions in Evolution*, ed. Edwin L. Wade (New York, 1986), pp. 143–55, pp. 151–2.

9 Pliny the Elder, *Natural History*, trans. H. Rackham (London, 1945), vol. IV, p. 501 (book 16, chapter 68).

10 Christoph Will, *International Basketry for Weavers and Collectors* (Exton, PA, 1985), p. 68; John Kennedy Melling, *Discovering London's Guilds and Liveries* (Princes Risborough, 2003), p. 42.

11 Maurice Bichard, *Baskets in Europe* (Abingdon, 2008), p. 43.

12 Kari Lønning, *The Art of Basketry* (New York, 2000), p. 88.

13 Kate Lynch, *A Guide to Somerset Willow: Past and Present* (Somerset, 2008), unpaginated.

14 Mary Butcher, *Contemporary International Basketmaking* (London, 1999), p. 16.

15 John Pickering, *A Greek and English Lexicon*, 3rd edn (Boston, 1832), p. 448; Peter Krentz, 'Warfare and Hoplites', in *The Cambridge Companion to Archaic Greece*, ed. H. A. Shapiro, pp. 61–84 (Cambridge, 2007), p. 69.

16 Will, *International Basketry*, p. 13.

17 Teiichi Yagashita, *Yanagi no bunkashi* (Kyoto, 1995), p. 211.

18 Chestnut, 'Plants Used by the Indians', p. 331; Paul D. Campbell, *Survival Skills in Native California* (Layton, UT, 1999), pp. 253–94.

19 Dieter Kuhn, *Chinese Baskets and Mats* (Wiesbaden, 1980).

20 Basil Hall Chamberlain and W. B. Mason, *A Handbook for Travellers in Japan*, 3rd edn (London, 1891), p. 11.

21 Yagashita, *Yanagi*, pp. 148–9.

22 Herodotus, *The Histories*, trans. Aubrey de Sélincourt, revd John Marincola (Harmondsworth, 1996), p. 77 (book 1, section 194).

23 Geoffrey Chaucer, *The Hous of Fame*, ed. Walter W. Skeat (Oxford, 1893), pp. 70–71.

24 Otto Lilienthal, *Birdflight as the Basis of Aviation*, trans. A. W. Isenthal (London, 1911), pp. xiv, 31, xiv.

25 Sir James Hall, 'On the Origin and Principles of Gothic Architecture', *Transactions of the Royal Society of Edinburgh*, 4 (1798), part 1, section 11, pp. 3–27, p. 12.

26 Ibid., pp. 13–19.

27 Ibid., pp. 19, 24–5.

28 Ibid., pp. 20, 27.

29 Sir James Hall, *Essay on the Origin, History, and Principles, of Gothic Architecture* (London, 1813), pp. 120, 125.

30 Simon Schama, *Landscape and Memory* (London, 1995), p. 236.

31 Hall, 'On the Origin', p. 8.

32 Edward Lebow, 'Patrick Dougherty', *American Craft*, LXV/3 (2005), pp. 32–7, p. 33.

33 Pat Summers, 'Itinerant Artist Patrick Dougherty', *Sculpture Magazine*, 11/6 (2005), pp. 53–7, p. 54.

34 Patrick Dougherty, *Stickwork* (New York, 2010), p. 118.

35 Pliny, *Natural History*, vol. IV, p. 501 (book 16, chapter 68).

36 Alexandra Croom, *Roman Furniture* (Stroud, 2007), pp. 116–17.

37 'Craftsman Willow Furniture', *The Craftsman*, XII/4 (1907), pp. 477–80, p. 478.

38 'Woven Willow Furniture from Germany', *The Craftsman Magazine*, XXI/5 (1912), pp. 578–9, p. 578.

39 'Craftsman Willow Furniture', p. 478.

40 Fiona MacCarthy, *William Morris: A Life for Our Time* (London, 1994), pp. 74, 674.

41 Linda Parry, *William Morris Textiles* (London, 1983), p. 42.

42 May Morris, 'Introduction', in *The Collected Works of William Morris* (New York, 1966), vol. XIII, pp. xiii–xxxvii, p. xxxii.

43 Caroline Arscott, *William Morris and Edward Burne-Jones: Interlacings* (New Haven, CT, 2008), pp. 136–7.

44 May Morris, *William Morris: Artist, Writer, Socialist* (New York, 1966), vol. I, p. 40.

45 Ibid., p. 36.

46 James Macaulay, *Charles Rennie Mackintosh* (New York, 2010), p. 210.

47 Thomas Howarth, *Charles Rennie Mackintosh and the Modern Movement* (London, 1952), p. 50.

48 Janice Helland, *The Studios of Frances and Margaret Macdonald* (Manchester, 1996), p. 131; Macaulay, *Charles Rennie Mackintosh*, p. 212.

49 'Ein Mackintosh-Teehaus in Glasgow', *Die Kunst*, 12 (1905), pp. 257–73, p. 270.

50 Howarth, *Charles Rennie Mackintosh*, p. 142.

3 Pattern of Romance and Mystery

1 Connie Rogers, *The Illustrated Encyclopedia of British Willow Ware* (Atglen, PA, 2004), pp. 373–82; Paul Christopher Scott, 'Ceramics and Landscape, Remediation and Confection: A Theory of Surface', PhD thesis (Manchester Metropolitan University), 2010, p. 72.

2 H. A. Crosby Forbes, *Hills and Streams: Landscape Decoration of Chinese Export and Blue and White Porcelain*, exh. cat., China Trade Museum, Milton, MA (Washington, DC, 1982), unpaginated.

3 David Quintner, *Willow! Solving the Mystery of Our 200-Year Love Affair with the Willow Pattern* (Burnstown, ON, 1997), pp. 169–70.

4 Charles Toogood Downing, *The Fan-qui in China* (London, 1838), vol. II, p. 83.

5 Robert L. Thorp and Richard Ellis Vinograd, *Chinese Art and Culture* (New York, 2001), p. 299.

6 Rogers, *Illustrated Encyclopedia*, p. 10.

7 Downing, *Fan-qui*, p. 84.

8 Robert Copeland, *Spode's Willow Pattern and Other Designs After the Chinese*, 3rd edn (London, 1999), p. 4.

9 For many years it was thought that Caughley had produced the first classic willow pattern china, but it is now accepted that Spode was the

first to offer it. Minton may have left Caughley to work for Spode and likely designed the willow pattern there.

10 Scott, 'Ceramics and Landscape', p. 18.

11 Thorp and Vinograd, *Chinese Art*, p. 344; Wang Gai et al., *The Mustard Seed Garden Manual of Painting*, trans. and ed. Mai-mai Sze (Princeton, NJ, 1977), p. III.

12 'The Pryor's Bank, Fulham', *Fraser's Magazine for Town and Country*, XXXII/192 (1845), pp. 631–46, p. 636.

13 Crosby Forbes, *Hills and Streams*, n.p.

14 William Churchill, review of *Chinesische Geschichte* by Heinrich Hermann, *Bulletin of the American Geographical Society*, XLVI/1 (1914), pp. 61–2, p. 61.

15 Charles Dickens, 'A Plated Article', *Household Words*, V/109 (1852), pp. 117–21, p. 120.

16 Warren E. Cox, *The Book of Pottery and Porcelain* (New York, 1944), vol. II, p. 769.

17 J.B.L., 'The Story of the Common Willow-Pattern Plate', *Family Friend*, I (1850), pp. 124–7, 151–4, p. 124.

18 *A Dish of Gossip Off the Willow Pattern, By Buz, and Plates to Match by Fuz* (London, 1867), p. 9; Mark Lemon, 'A True History of the Celebrated Wedgewood [*sic*] Hieroglyph, Commonly Called the Willow Pattern', *Bentley's Miscellany*, 3 (1838), pp. 61–5, p. 62.

19 Dickens, 'Plated Article', p. 120.

20 Quintner, *Willow!*, pp. 85, 46, 72, 48.

21 Lemon, 'True History', p. 65.

22 J.B.L., 'Story', pp. 126, 127, 154.

23 Patricia O'Hara, '"The Willow Pattern that We Knew": The Victorian Literature of Blue Willow', *Victorian Studies*, XXXVI/4 (1993), pp. 421–42, p. 426.

24 John Henry Newman, *Loss and Gain: The Story of a Convert* [1848], 6th edn (London, 1874), p. 76.

25 Letter of 4 March 1900 from Woodford to Charles Read of the British Museum.

26 Quintner, *Willow*, pp. 21, 129; John R. Haddad, 'Imagined Journeys to Distant Cathay: Constructing China with Ceramics, 1780–1920', *Winterthur Portfolio*, XLI/1 (2007), pp. 53–80, pp. 65–6.

27 Lemon, 'True History', pp. 62, 63.

28 Dickens, 'Plated Article', p. 120.

29 *Dish of Gossip*, p. 7.

30 Henry Wadsworth Longfellow, *Kéramos and Other Poems* (Boston, 1878), pp. 3–25, pp. 20–21.

31 J.B.L., 'Story', p. 124.

32 Dickens, 'Plated Article', p. 118.

33 J.B.L., 'Story', p. 124.

34 *The Mandarin's Daughter! Being the Simple Story of the Willow-Pattern Plate* (London, 1865), p. 23.

35 'Theatres and Music', *The Spectator*, XXV/1228 (1852), p. 30.

36 Elizabeth Hope Chang, *Britain's Chinese Eye: Literature, Empire, and Aesthetics in Nineteenth-Century Britain* (Stanford, CA, 2010), p. 89.

37 Anne Anderson, '"Fearful Consequences . . . of Living Up to One's Teapot": Men, Women, and "Cultchah" in the English Aesthetic Movement *c.* 1870–1900', *Victorian Literature and Culture*, 37 (2009), pp. 219–54, p. 236.

38 George Meredith, *The Egoist: A Comedy in Narrative*, ed. Lionel Stevenson (Boston, 1958), pp. 35, 74, 126, 282, 197.

39 Ibid., p. 283.

40 Ibid., pp. 330, 23.

41 O'Hara, '"Willow Pattern"', p. 431.

42 Robert van Gulik, *The Willow Pattern: A Chinese Detective Story* (London, 1965).

43 W. J. Burley, *Death in Willow Pattern* (New York, 1969).

44 James Merrill, 'The Willowware Cup', in *Braving the Elements* (New York, 1972), p. 36.

45 James Merrill, 'Mirabell: Book 3', in *The Changing Light at Sandover* (New York, 2006), p. 152.

46 Linda Sandino, 'Print and Be Damned', *Studio Pottery Magazine* (1996–7), pp. 30–33, p. 32.

47 *Breaking the Mould: New Approaches to Ceramics* (London, 2007), p. 190.

48 Paul Scott, *Painted Clay: Graphic Arts and the Ceramic Surface* (London, 2001), p. 147.

49 Quoted in Mark Thompson, *Gerry Wedd: Thong Cycle* (Kent Town, S. Australia, 2008), n.p.

50 'Arita Porcelain', *Oriental Economist*, XXXIII/182 (1946), p. 306.

51 Antony Hudek and Conrad Atkinson, 'Excavating the Body Politic: An Interview with Conrad Atkinson', *Art Journal*, LXII/2 (2003), pp. 4–21, pp. 4–5.

52 Quintner, *Willow*, p. 126.

53 Red Weldon Sandlin, 'About the Artist', www.ferringallery.com, accessed 23 February 2012.

4 Tree of Prose and Poetry

1 Theophrastus, *Enquiry into Plants and Minor Works on Odours and Weather Signs*, trans. Sir Arthur Hort (London, 1916), vol. I, p. 249.

2 Roman Jakobson, 'Closing Statement: Linguistics and Poetics', in *Style in Language*, ed. Thomas A. Sebeok (Cambridge, MA, 1966), pp. 350–77, pp. 370–71.

3 Gaston Bachelard, *Water and Dreams: An Essay on the Imagination of Matter*, trans. Edith R. Farrell (Dallas, TX, 1983), p. 184.

4 François-René de Chateaubriand, *Mémoires d'Outre-Tombe* (Paris, 1997), vol. I, p. 208.

5 Princess Marthe Bibesco, *Isvor: The Country of Willows*, trans. Hamish Miles (London, 1924), pp. 4, 165.

6   Patricia Bjaaland Welch, *Chinese Art: A Guide to Motifs and Visual Imagery*
    (Tokyo, 2008), p. 40.

7   Liu Yü-hsi, 'Willow Branch Song', trans. Daniel Bryant, in *Sunflower
    Splendor: Three Thousand Years of Chinese Poetry*, ed. Wu-chi Liu and Irving
    Yucheng Lo (Bloomington, IN, 1975), p. 200.

8   Wolfram Eberhard, *A Dictionary of Chinese Symbols: Hidden Symbols in Chinese
    Life and Thought*, trans. G. L. Campbell (London, 1986), p. 314.

9   Li Shangyin, 'Willow', in *Poems of the Late T'ang*, trans. A. C. Graham
    (Harmondsworth, 1977), p. 154.

10 Yang Yuhuan, 'For my Maidservant Zhang Yunrong, upon Seeing Her
    Dance', in *Willow, Wine, Mirror, Moon: Women's Poems from Tang China*, trans.
    Jeanne Larsen (Rochester, NY, 2005), p. 33.

11 Harriet Zurndorfer, 'Willowy as a Willow', in *100,000 Years of Beauty*, ed.
    Elisabeth Azoulay (Paris, 2009), vol. III, p. 114; Eberhard, *Dictionary*,
    p. 314.

12 Jerome Silbergeld, 'Kung Hsien's Self-portrait in Willows, with Notes
    on the Willow in Chinese Painting and Literature', *Artibus Asiae*, XLII/1
    (1980), pp. 5–38, p. 25; Eberhard, *Dictionary*, p. 314.

13 Marsha L. Wagner, *The Lotus Boat: The Origins of Chinese Tz'u Poetry in T'ang
    Popular Culture* (New York, 1984), pp. 101–02.

14 Ibid., p. 86.

15 Eberhard, *Dictionary*, p. 314.

16 Liu Yü-hsi, 'Willow Branch Song', p. 200.

17 Michelle Mi-Hsi Yeh, 'The Chinese Poem: The Visible and the Invisible
    in Chinese Poetry', *Manoa*, XII/1 (2000), pp. 139–46, p. 141.

18 Silbergeld, 'Kung Hsien's Self-Portrait', p. 26.

19 Zhou Dehua, 'Willow Branches', in *Willow, Wine, Mirror, Moon*, p. 92.

20 Su Shih, 'After Chang Chi-fu's Lyric on the Willow Catkin: Using the
    Same Rhyming Words', trans. James J. Y. Liu, in *Sunflower Splendor*, p. 350.

21 Teiichi Yagashita, *Yanagi no bunkashi* (Kyoto, 1995), p. 28; Silbergeld, 'Kung
    Hsien's Self-Portrait', p. 25.

22 Sei Shōnagon, *The Pillow Book*, trans. Meredith McKinney (London,
    2006), p. 87.

23 Andrew Lawrence Markus, *The Willow in Autumn: Ryūtei Tanehiko, 1783–1842*
    (Cambridge, MA, 1992), p. 38; Robin D. Gill, *The Woman Without a Hole and
    Other Risky Themes from Old Japanese Poems: 18–19c senryū compiled, translated and
    essayed* (Key Biscayne, FL, 2007), p. 468.

24 Yagashita, *Yanagi*, p. 29.

25 *The Moon in the Pines: Zen Haiku*, trans. Jonathan Clements (London,
    2000), p. 31.

26 Yagashita, *Yanagi*, p. 140.

27 Makoto Ueda, *The Path of Flowering Thorn: The Life and Poetry of Yosa Buson*
    (Stanford, CA, 1998), p. 101.

28 Yagishita, *Yanagi*, pp. 70, 66, 205, 207.

29 See, for example, Lafcadio Hearn, *Kwaidan: Stories and Studies of Strange Things*
    (Boston, 1904), pp. 65–75.

30 Nizami Ganjavi, *The Loves of Lailí and Majnún*, trans. James Atkinson (London, 1894).

31 Pausanias, *The Description of Greece*, trans. Thomas Taylor (London, 1794), vol. III, p. 187.

32 Rainer Maria Rilke, *Die Sonette an Orpheus: geschrieben als ein Grab-mal für Wera Ouckama Knoop* (Leipzig, 1923), p. 12.

33 See Karl Siegler, 'Translations of Rilke's "Sonnets to Orpheus" with Pertinent Critical and Textual Commentary', MA thesis (Simon Fraser University, 1974), p. 60.

34 Claudette Sartiliot, *Herbarium Verbarium: The Discourse of Flowers* (Lincoln, NE, 1993), p. 71.

35 Virgil, *The Eclogues of Virgil*, trans. David Ferry (New York, 1999), pp. 81, 7, 9.

36 Robert Herrick, 'To the Willow-tree', in *Hesperides; or, The Works Both Humane and Divine of Robert Herrick Esq.* (London, 1648), p. 120, lines 5–8.

37 Eamon Grennan, 'The Women's Voices in "Othello": Speech, Song, Silence', *Shakespeare Quarterly*, XXXVIII/3 (1987), pp. 275–92, p. 277; Ernest Brennecke, '"Nay, That's Not Next!": The Significance of Desdemona's "Willow Song"', *Shakespeare Quarterly*, IV/I (1953), pp. 35–8, p. 35.

38 Frank Kermode, 'Othello, the Moor of Venice', in *The Riverside Shakespeare*, ed. G. Blakemore Evans and J.J.M. Tobin, 2nd edn (Boston, 1997), pp. 1246–50, p. 1246.

39 Joel Fineman, 'The Sound of O in Othello: The Real of the Tragedy of Desire', in *The Subjectivity Effect in Western Literary Tradition: Essays Toward the Release of Shakespeare's Will* (Cambridge, MA, 1991), pp. 143–64, pp. 145, 151, 157, 158.

40 Kimberly Rhodes, *Ophelia and Victorian Visual Culture: Representing Body Politics in the Nineteenth Century* (Aldershot, 2008), p. 74; 'Exhibition of the Royal Academy', *The Times* (1 May 1852), p. 8.

41 Dante Gabriel Rossetti, 'Willowwood', in *Poems* (London, 1870), pp. 212–15.

42 Isobel Armstrong, 'D. G. Rossetti and Christina Rossetti as Sonnet Writers', *Victorian Poetry*, XLVIII/4 (2010), pp. 461–73, esp. pp. 466–7.

43 Christina Rossetti, 'An Echo from Willowwood', *Magazine of Art* (1890), p. 385.

44 W. H. Auden, 'Underneath an Abject Willow', in *The English Auden: Poems, Essays and Dramatic Writings, 1927–1939*, ed. Edward Mendelson (London, 1977), p. 160.

45 Hans Christian Andersen, 'Under the Willow Tree', in *The Complete Fairy Tales and Stories*, trans. Erik Christian Haugaard (New York, 1983), pp. 431–44, pp. 443, 444.

46 Letter to Fritz Lieber of 9 November 1936, in *Fritz Lieber and H. P. Lovecraft: Writers of the Dark*, ed. Ben J. S. Szumskyj and S. T. Joshi (Holicong, NJ, 2004), p. 15.

47 Algernon Blackwood, 'The Willows', in *The Listener, and Other Stories* (London, 1907), pp. 127–203, pp. 127, 130, 146–7, 186, 153.

48 J.R.R. Tolkien, *The Lord of the Rings* (London, 1993), pp. 111–17.

49 Ibid., pp. 121–8.

50 J. K. Rowling, *Harry Potter and the Chamber of Secrets* (New York, 1999), pp. 75, 89.

51 J. K. Rowling, *Harry Potter and the Prisoner of Azkaban* (New York, 1999), p. 335.

52 Noel Chevalier, 'The Liberty Tree and the Whomping Willow: Political Justice, Magical Science, and Harry Potter', *The Lion and the Unicorn*, XXIX/3 (2005), pp. 397–415, p. 402.

53 Letter of 2 September 1908 from Algernon Methuen to Kenneth Grahame, quoted in Kenneth Grahame, *The Annotated Wind in the Willows*, ed. Annie Gauger (New York, 2009), p. lvi.

54 Grahame, *Annotated Wind*, pp. 171–2.

55 Hubert Selby Jr, *The Willow Tree* (New York, 1998), p. 133.

56 Carolyn Forché, 'The Garden Shukkei-en', in *The Angel of History* (New York, 1994), pp. 70–71.

57 Velimir Khlebnikov, 'The Willow Twig', in *Collected Works of Velimir Khlebnikov*, trans. Paul Schmidt, ed. Ronald Vroon (Cambridge, MA, 1989), vol. II, pp. 150–51.

5 Brushes with Fame

1 Richard Edwards, *The Heart of Ma Yuan: The Search for a Southern Song Aesthetic* (Hong Kong, 2011), p. 7.

2 Sherman E. Lee and Wen Fong, 'Streams and Mountains without End: A Northern Sung Handscroll and Its Significance in the History of Early Chinese Painting', revd edn, *Artibus Asiae, Supplementum*, 14 (1967), pp. 1–59, p. 24.

3 Edwards, *Heart of Ma Yuan*, p. 222.

4 Ibid.

5 Jerome Silbergeld, 'Kung Hsien's Self-Portrait in Willows, with Notes on the Willow in Chinese Painting and Literature', *Artibus Asiae*, XLII/I (1980), pp. 5–38, p. 33.

6 Edwards, *Heart of Ma Yuan*, p. 222.

7 Patricia Bjaaland Welch, *Chinese Art: A Guide to Motifs and Visual Imagery* (Tokyo, 2008), p. 252.

8 Wang Gai et al., *The Mustard Seed Garden Manual of Painting*, trans. and ed. Mai-mai Sze (Princeton, NJ, 1977), p. 114.

9 Quoted in Silbergeld, 'Kung Hsien's Self-Portrait', p. 32.

10 Wang, *Mustard Seed*, p. 111.

11 Sebastian Izzard, *Hiroshige / Eisen: The Sixty-Nine Stations of the Kisokaido* (New York, 2008), p. 78.

12 Amina Okada, *Le Grand Moghol et ses peintres: miniaturistes de l'Inde aux XVIe et XVIIe Siècles* (Paris, 1992), pp. 105–6.

13 William Gilpin, *Remarks on Forest Scenery, and Other Woodland Views*, ed. Sir Thomas Dick Lauder (Edinburgh, 1834), vol. I, p. 133.

14 Jacob George Strutt, *Sylva Britannica; or, Portraits of Forest Trees Distinguished for their Antiquity, Magnitude, or Beauty* (London, 1830), p. 98.

15 Letter from Vincent van Gogh to Theo van Gogh, written between 12 and 15 October 1881, inv. no. b172 V/1961 in the Van Gogh Museum, Amsterdam.

16 Stephanie S. Dickey, '"Judicious Negligence": Rembrandt Transforms an Emblematic Convention', *Art Bulletin*, LXVIII/2 (1986), pp. 253–62, p. 256.

17 Susan Donahue Kuretsky, 'Rembrandt's Tree Stump: An Iconographic Attribute of St Jerome', *Art Bulletin*, LVI/4 (1974), pp. 571–80, pp. 571, 580.

18 Kenneth Clark, *Landscape into Art*, revd edn (London, 1979), p. 124.

19 *Claude Gellée, dit le Lorrain: le dessinateur face à la nature*, ed. Carel van Tuyll van Serooskerken and Michiel C. Plomp, exh. cat., Musée du Louvre, Paris, and Teylers Museum, Haarlem (Paris, 2011), p. 266.

20 John Constable, quoted in Edward Verrall Lucas, *John Constable, the Painter* (London, 1924), p. 57.

21 Letter from John Constable to Rev. John Fisher, 23 October 1821, in *John Constable's Correspondence*, ed. R. B. Beckett (Ipswich, 1968), vol. VI, p. 77.

22 J. Ernest Phythian, *Trees in Nature, Myth and Art* (London, 1907), p. 90.

23 Marius de Zayas, *How, When, and Why Modern Art Came to New York*, ed. Francis M. Naumann (Cambridge, MA, 1996), p. 2.

24 J. B. Kerfoot, 'Black Art: A Lecture on Necromancy and the Photo-Secession', *Camera Work*, 8 (1904), reprinted in *Camera Work: A Critical Anthology*, ed. Jonathan Green (New York, 1973), pp. 47–9, p. 49.

25 *The Alternative Image: An Aesthetic and Technical Exploration of Nonconventional Photographic Printing Processes*, exh. cat., John Michael Kohler Arts Centre, Sheboygan, WI, and Toledo Museum of Art, OH (Sheboygan, WI, 1983), p. 56.

26 Gustave Geffroy, *Claude Monet: sa vie, son temps, son oeuvre* (Paris, 1922), p. 336.

27 Virginia Spate and David Bromfield, 'A New and Strange Beauty: Monet and Japanese Art', in *Monet and Japan*, exh. cat., National Gallery of Australia, Canberra (Canberra, 2001), pp. 2–63, p. 51.

28 Virginia Spate, *The Colour of Time: Claude Monet* (London, 1992), p. 310; see also Steven Z. Levine, *Monet, Narcissus, and Self-Reflection: The Modernist Myth of the Self* (Chicago, 1994).

29 Maurice Rollinat, 'Le Saule', in *Paysages et paysans: Poésies* (Paris, 1899), p. 37.

30 Spate, *Colour of Time*, p. 314.

31 Clare A. P. Willsdon, *In the Gardens of Impressionism* (New York, 2004), p. 229.

32 Roger Marx, 'Les "Nymphéas" de M. Claude Monet', *Gazette des Beaux-Arts*, 624 (1909), pp. 523–31, p. 529.

33 Spate, *Colour of Time*, pp. 284, 306.

34 Willsdon, *Gardens of Impressionism*, p. 229.

35 Spate, *Colour of Time*, p. 303.
36 Ibid., p. 306.
37 Gaston Bachelard, *Water and Dreams: An Essay on the Imagination of Matter*, trans. Edith R. Farrell (Dallas, TX, 1983), p. 92.
38 Spate, *Colour of Time*, p. 307.
39 Louis Gillet, *Trois variations sur Claude Monet* (Paris, 1927), p. 106.
40 Spate, *Colour of Time*, p. 314.
41 Levine, *Monet, Narcissus, and Self-Reflection*, pp. 191, 258.
42 Spate, *Colour of Time*, p. 307.
43 Andrew Marvell, 'Eyes and Tears', in *Andrew Marvell*, ed. Frank Kermode and Keith Walker (Oxford, 1992), p. 16, lines 54–6.

Conclusion: Willow in the World Garden

1 'Pope's Villa', *The Topographer*, I/8 (1789), pp. 470–74, p. 472.
2 Charles M. Skinner, *Myths and Legends of Flowers, Trees, Fruits, and Plants in All Ages and All Climes* (Philadelphia, PA, 1925), p. 298.
3 David Quintner, *Willow! Solving the Mystery of Our 200-Year Love Affair with the Willow Pattern* (Burnstown, ON, 1997), pp. 52–3.
4 Quoted in Anthony Beckles Wilson, 'Pope's Grotto in Twickenham', *Garden History*, XXVI/I (1998), pp. 31–59, p. 55.
5 Archie Miles, *Silva: The Tree in Britain* (London, 1999), p. 192.
6 Robert L. Thorp and Richard Ellis Vinograd, *Chinese Art and Culture* (New York, 2001), p. 360.
7 John Russell, Duke of Bedford, 'Introduction', in James Forbes, *Salictum Woburnense: or, A Catalogue of Willows, Indigenous and Foreign, in the Collection of the Duke of Bedford, Woburn Abbey* (London, 1829), p. iv.
8 William Gilpin, *Remarks on Forest Scenery, and Other Woodland Views*, ed. Sir Thomas Dick Lauder (Edinburgh, 1834), vol. I, p. 133.
9 Alexander de Humboldt, *Political Essay on the Kingdom of New Spain*, vol. II (London, 1811), pp. 96–100.
10 Dana Leibsohn, *Script and Glyph: Pre-Hispanic History, Colonial Bookmaking and the Histoira Tolteca-Chichimeca* (Washington, DC, 2009), p. 116.
11 Philip L. Crossley, 'Just Beyond the Eye: Floating Gardens in Aztec Mexico', *Historical Geography*, vol. XXXII (2004), pp. 111–35.
12 See John Warnes, *Living Willow Sculpture* (Tunbridge Wells, 2002).
13 Alessandro Rocca, *Natural Architecture* (New York, 2007), p. 65.
14 Carolyn Forché, 'The Garden Shukkei-en', in *The Angel of History* (New York, 1994), pp. 70–71.

Further Reading

Bibesco, Princess Marthe, *Isvor: The Country of Willows*, trans. Hamish Miles (London, 1924)

Bichard, Maurice, *Baskets in Europe* (Abingdon, 2008)

Blackwood, Algernon, 'The Willows', in *The Listener, and Other Stories* (London, 1907)

Chang, Elizabeth Hope, *Britain's Chinese Eye: Literature, Empire and Aesthetics in Nineteenth-Century Britain* (Stanford, CA, 2010)

Copeland, Robert, *Spode's Willow Pattern and Other Designs after the Chinese*, 3rd edn (London, 1999)

Culpeper, William, *Culpeper's English Physician; and Complete Herbal* (London, 1789)

Dougherty, Patrick, *Stickwork* (New York, 2010)

Edmonds, Richard L., 'The Willow Palisade', *Annals of the Association of American Geographers*, LXIX/4 (1979), pp. 569–621

Edwards, Richard, *The Heart of Ma Yuan: The Search for a Southern Song Aesthetic* (Hong Kong, 2011)

Evelyn, John, *Sylva; or, A Discourse of Forest-Trees* (London, 1670)

Forbes, James, *Salictum Woburnense; or, A Catalogue of Willows, Indigenous and Foreign, in the Collection of the Duke of Bedford, Woburn Abbey* (London, 1829)

Frazer, Sir James, *The Golden Bough: A Study in Magic and Religion*, abbreviated edn (New York, 1996)

Gerard, John, *The Herbal; or, Generall historie of plantes* (London, 1597)

Graham, A. C., trans., *Poems of the Late T'ang* (Harmondsworth, 1977)

Grahame, Kenneth, *The Annotated Wind in the Willows*, ed. Annie Gauger (New York, 2009)

Gubernatis, Angelo de, *La Mythologie des plantes; ou, Les Légendes du règne végétal* (Paris, 1882)

Hall, Sir James, *Essay on the Origin, History, and Principles, of Gothic Architecture* (London, 1813)

—, 'On the Origin and Principles of Gothic Architecture', *Transactions of the Royal Society of Edinburgh*, 4 (1798), part I, section II, pp. 3–27

Hanley, S. J., 'Willow', in *Energy Crops*, ed. Nigel G. Halford and Angela Carp

(Cambridge, 2011), pp. 259–74

Hooker, William Jackson, *The British Flora; comprising the Phaenogamous, or Flowering Plants, and the Ferns*, 2nd edn (London, 1831)

Keimer, Ludwig, 'L'arbre tjeret: est il réellement le saule égyptien (*Salix safsaf* Forsk.)?', *Bulletin de l'Institut français d'archéologie orientale*, 31 (1931), pp. 177–237

Khlebnikov, Velimir, 'The Willow Twig', in *Collected Works of Velimir Khlevnikov*, trans. Paul Schmidt, ed. Ronald Vroon (Cambridge, MA, 1989), vol. II, pp. 150–51

L., J. B., 'The Story of the Common Willow-Pattern Plate', *The Family Friend*, 1 (1850), pp. 124–7, 151–4

Larsen, Jeanne, trans., *Willow, Wine, Mirror, Moon: Women's Poems from Tang China* (Rochester, NY, 2005)

Lemon, Mark, 'A True History of the Celebrated Wedgewood [*sic*] Hieroglyph, Commonly Called the Willow Pattern', *Bentley's Miscellany*, 3 (1838), pp. 61–5

Levine, Steven Z., *Monet, Narcissus and Self-Reflection: The Modernist Myth of the Self* (Chicago, 1994)

Lilienthal, Otto, *Birdflight as the Basis of Aviation*, trans. A. W. Isenthal (London, 1911)

Liu, Wu-chi, and Irving Yucheng Lo, eds, *Sunflower Splendor: Three Thousand Years of Chinese Poetry* (Bloomington, IN, 1975)

Lynch, Kate, *Willow: Paintings and Drawings of Somerset Voices*, rev. edn (S.I., 2005)

Mannhardt, Wilhelm, *Der Baumkultus der Germanen und ihrer Nachbarstämme* (Berlin, 1875)

Markus, Andrew Lawrence, *The Willow in Autumn: Ryūtei Tanehiko, 1783–1842* (Cambridge, MA, 1992)

Meredith, George, *The Egoist: A Comedy in Narrative*, ed. Lionel Stevenson (Boston, MA, 1958)

Miles, Archie, *Silva: The Tree in Britain* (London, 1999)

Newsholme, Christopher, *Willows: The Genus* Salix (London, 1992)

O'Hara, Patricia, '"The Willow Pattern that We Knew": The Victorian Literature of Blue Willow', *Victorian Studies*, XXXVI/4 (1993), pp. 421–42

Phythian, J. Ernest, *Trees in Nature, Myth and Art* (London, 1907)

Quintner, David Richard, *Willow! Solving the Mystery of our 200-Year Love Affair with the Willow Pattern* (Burnstown, ON, 1997)

Rahner, Hugo, *Greek Myths and Christian Mystery* (London, 1963)

Rogers, Connie, *The Illustrated Encyclopedia of British Willow Ware* (Atglen, PA, 2004)

Sammes, Aylett, *Britannia Antiqua Illustrata; or, The Antiquities of Ancient Britain* (London, 1676)

Shanks, Ralph, *Indian Baskets of Central California: Art, Culture and History*, ed. Lisa Woo Shanks (Novato, CA, 2006)

Silbergeld, Jerome, 'Kung Hsien's Self-Portrait in Willows, with Notes on the Willow in Chinese Painting and Literature', *Artibus Asiae*, XLII/1 (1980), pp. 5–38

Skinner, Charles M., *Myths and Legends of Flowers, Trees, Fruits and Plants in All Ages and All Climes* (Philadelphia, PA, 1925)

Spate, Virginia, *The Colour of Time: Claude Monet* (London, 1992)

Stone, Edmund, 'An Account of the Success of the Bark of the Willow in the Cure of Agues', *Philosophical Transactions of the Royal Society of London*, 53 (1763), pp. 195–200

Thoreau, Henry David, *Faith in a Seed: The Dispersion of Seeds and Other Late Natural History Writings*, ed. Bradley P. Dean (Washington, DC, 1993)

Warnes, John, *Living Willow Sculpture* (Tunbridge Wells, 2000)

Will, Christoph, *International Basketry for Weavers and Collectors* (Exton, PA, 1985)

Wurges, Jennifer, and Rebecca J. Frey, 'White Willow', in *The Gale Encyclopedia of Alternative Medicine*, 3rd edn (Detroit, MI, 2009), vol. IV, pp. 2375–7

Wyckoff, Lydia L., ed., *Woven Worlds: Basketry from the Clark Field Collection at the Philbrook Museum of Art* (Tulsa, OK, 2001)

Yagashita, Teiichi, *Yanagi no bunkashi* (Kyoto, 1995)

Zurndorfer, Harriet, 'Willowy as a Willow', in *100,000 Years of Beauty*, ed. Elisabeth Azoulay (Paris, 2009), vol. III, pp. 113–14

Associations and Websites

CONRAD ATKINSON
www.conradatkinson.com

THE BASKETMAKERS' ASSOCIATION
www.basketassoc.org

LISE BECH
www.bechbaskets.net

CALIFORNIA INDIAN BASKETWEAVERS ASSOCATION
www.ciba.org/index.php

JOAN CARRIGAN
www.joancarrigan.com

CENTRAL YUKON SPECIES INVENTORY PROJECT
www.flora.dempstercountry.org

ADRIAN CHARLTON
www.norfolkbaskets.co.uk

THE CHINAMPAS OF MEXICO
www.chinampas.info

DANISH WILLOW ASSOCIATION
www.pileforeningen.dk

ROBERT DAWSON
www.aestheticsabotage.com

DAVID DREW
www.vannerie.com

SERENA DE LA HEY
www.serenadelahey.com

ALASTAIR HESELTINE
www.alastairheseltine.com

ANNE METTE HJØRNHOLMS
www.hjornholm.dk

JOE HOGAN BASKETS
www.joehoganbaskets.com

CHARLES KRAFFT
www.antiquesatoz.com/artatoz/krafft

TREVOR LEAT AND ALEX RIGG
www.leatrigg.com

KATHERINE LEWIS
www.dunbargardens.com

KATE LYNCH
www.katelynch.co.uk

STEEN H. MADSEN
www.steen-madsen.dk

NORTHWEST NATIVE AMERICAN BASKETWEAVERS ASSOCIATION
www.nnaba.org

SANFTE STRUKTUREN
www.sanftestrukturen.de/Weidenbau/Weidenbau.html

PAUL SCOTT
www.cumbrianblues.com

SCOTTISH BASKETMAKERS' CIRCLE
www.scottishbasketmakerscircle.com

EVA SEIDENFADEN
www.vissinggaard.dk

RED WELDON SANDLIN
wwwwww.ferringallery.com

Acknowledgements

I am grateful to all the artists, basketmakers, collectors, curators, musicians, naturalists, photographers, scholars and willow growers who helped me with this project, including Conrad Atkinson, Jordan Bear, Lise Bech, Conrad Biernacki, Joan Carrigan, Lya Cattel, Simon Chadwick, Adrian Charlton, Philip Crossley, Robert Dawson, Ulysses Dietz, Patrick Dougherty, David and Judy Drew, James Ellison, Anne Folehave, Peter Ganser, Meredith Hale, Joe Hogan, Carl Knappett, Emma Kosonen, Charles Krafft, Katherine Lewis, Trevor Leat, Elizabeth Legge, Steve Lospalluto, Kate Lynch, Meredith Martin, George Meanwell, Jordan Metzgar, Thalat Monajemi, Natasha Myers, Ermira Najacaj, Kim Northrop, Salvatore Prudente, Vanfei Qiu, Shabnam Rahimi-Golkhandan, Lene Rasmussen, Alex Rigg, Karen Ryan, Mana Sadeghipour, Dorion Sagan, Linda Sandino, Red Weldon Sandlin, Benjamin Schott, Paul Scott, Alasdair Syme, John Tyler, Horst Wiedermann, Anthony Wu and Yang Zheng. I thank my research assistants Elizabeth Parke, Sara Osenton and Ikumi Yoshida-Roleinghoff for their help with Chinese and Japanese texts. As always, my greatest debts are to Holger Syme and Miranda Purves for their invaluable support and critical eyes.

Photo Acknowledgements

✻

The author and publishers wish to express their thanks to the below sources of illustrative material and / or permission to reproduce it.

Photo © Charles Addams, with permission Tee and Charles Addams Foundation: p. 127; courtesy of Albert and Shirley Small Special Collections Library, University of Virginia: p. 195; photo courtesy of Lise Bech, © Shannon Tofts: p. 72; photos courtesy of and © Bibliothèque nationale de France: pp. 20 (MS LATIN 9474, fol. 150v), 47, 198 (MS MEXICAIN 46–58, p. 25); photos courtesy of Conrad Biernacki: pp. 103, 107 (left); photo © 2009 Bonhams & Butterfields Auctioneers Corp. All Rights Reserved: p. 93; photos courtesy of and © Bridgeman Art Library: pp. 98 (Glasgow Museums), 155 (Delaware Art Museum, Samuel and Mary R. Bancroft Memorial, 1935); photos © Trustees of the British Museum: pp. 36, 37, 48, 51 (photo by James Edge-Partington), 107 (right), 113 (left and right), 147, 174, 177, 178, 196; photo courtesy of Joan Carrigan, by Janet Dwyer: p. 72; photos courtesy of Patrick Dougherty, © Rob Cardillo, © Nell Campbell: pp. 89, 90; photo courtesy of and © Philip Crossley: p. 199; photo © Alfredo Dagli Orti / The Art Archive at Art Resource, NY: p. 31; photo courtesy of and © Gianni Dagli Orti / The Art Archive at Art Resource, NY: p. 92; photos courtesy of Robert Dawson: pp. 121, 122; photo courtesy of and © James Ellison: p. 10; photo by Eleanore Hopper, courtesy of Ronald Feldman Fine Arts, New York: p. 128; photo courtesy of Anne Folehave: p. 73; photos courtesy of and © Peter Ganser: pp. 204 (top and bottom), 205; photo courtesy of Joe Hogan: p. 73; photos courtesy of Imperial War Museum, London, © IWM (FEQ 813), (COM 59): pp. 75, 76; photos courtesy of Lya_Cattel, cunfek/iStockphoto: pp. 13 (top), 15 (top); photo © Markku Kosonen, courtesy of Emma Kosonen: p. 74; photo courtesy of and © Trevor Leat: p. 57; photos courtesy of and © Erich Lessing / Art Resource, NY: pp. 66 (Musée d'Archéologie Nationale, Saint-Germain-en-Laye, France), 186 (Galerie Larock-Granoff, Paris); photos courtesy of Library of Congress, Washington, DC: pp. 70 (P. H. Emerson, *Pictures of East Anglian Life* [London, 1888], plate XIV), 78 (top and bottom), 81, 141 (also with permission of the artist's estate), 171; photo courtesy of and © Kate Lynch: p. 69; photo courtesy of and © Jordan Metzgar: p. 15

(bottom); photo by Andrea Moro: p. 194; photographs © 2012 Museum of Fine Arts, Boston: pp. 68 (The Elizabeth Day McCormick Collection, 44.184), 106 (gift of Miss Gertrude Townsend, RES.59.21), 136 (Special Chinese and Japanese Fund, 28.840), 142–3 (William S. and John T. Spaulding Collection, 21.9987), 167 (Special Chinese and Japanese Fund, 14.61), 175 (Francis Bartlett Donation of 1912 and Picture Fund, 14.609); photo © The Museum of Modern Art, New York / Licensed by SCALA / Art Resource, NY: p. 185; photos © Newark Museum / Art Resource, NY: pp. 64, 131; photo courtesy of and © Kim Northrop: p. 203 (top); photo © 2012 Philbrook Museum of Art, Inc., Tulsa, OK: p. 65 (Philbrook Museum of Art, gift of Clark Field, 1942.14.1909); photo © Pitt Rivers Museum, Oxford: p. 43; photo courtesy of and © Salvatore Prudente: p. 9; photo courtesy of and © Vanfei Qiu: p. 27; photo courtesy of and © Lene Rasmussen: p. 19; photos © Réunion des Musées Nationaux / Art Resource, NY: pp. 182–3 (Musée d'Orsay), 190–91 (Musée de l'Orangerie); RIBA Library Drawings Collection, photo courtesy of Royal Institute of British Architects, London: pp. 86–7; photo courtesy of Karen Ryan: p. 123; photo courtesy of and © Harriet Rycroft: p. 203 (bottom); photo courtesy of Sam Noble Oklahoma Museum of Natural History: p. 63; photo courtesy of and © Benjamin Schott: p. 33; photo courtesy of Science Museum, London: p. 26; photos courtesy of and © Paul Scott: pp. 124, 125; photo courtesy of Yuri Silagin: p. 130; photo by Gael Simon: pp. 200–1; photo courtesy of Studiocanal Films: p. 56; photo © Tate, London: pp. 150–51; photos courtesy of the Toronto Public Libraries: pp. 54, 160, 161; photos courtesy of and © John Tyler: pp. 6, 13 (bottom), 14, 22; photos courtesy of the University of Toronto libraries: pp. 17 (left and right), 24, 30, 44, 53, 67, 80, 82, 83, 84, 85, 97, 99, 116, 170; photo courtesy of the Velimir Khlebnikov Museum, Astrakhan, Russia: p. 164; photos © Victoria & Albert Museum, London: pp. 38, 41, 79, 95, 96 (top and bottom), 108, 181; photo courtesy of and © Yang Zheng: p. 12. All other photos are by the author and/or are in the public domain.

Index